Welcome to Our Table

Ménière's *Low-Sodium* Cookbook
The *Art* of Flavour

*Proudly created by people with Ménière's Disease.
Profits donated to Ménière's research.*

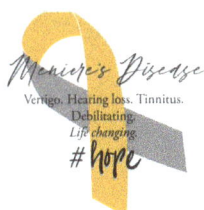

Welcome to Our Table ~ Ménière's *Low-Sodium* Cookbook
© 2025 Julieann Wallace & *Lilly Pilly Publishing*

A book of recipes and low-sodium ideas from people living with Ménière's disease, collated by Julieann Wallace, in collaboration with Sally Edsall, Kim Dean, Anne Elias, and Phillip Stephanou.

All rights reserved.

No part of this publication may be reproduced, stored in a retrieval system or transmitted, in any form or by any means, electronic, mechanical, photocopying, recording or otherwise, without prior written permission of the copyright holder, including for training of bloody AI.

This book does not replace the advice of a medical professional. Consult your physician before making any changes to your diet or regular health plan. *While every effort has been made to ensure recipes are low-sodium, you may still have vertigo and other symptoms due to other anomalies that contribute to symptoms, such as weather, stress, other foods, etc.*

Any medical information and advise is based on medical research papers, and not the hallucinating Artificial Intelligence.

Recipe legalities: The recipes contained in this book are not exact copies of recipes found on the Internet, or in cookbooks, but come from people who have tried and tested and *reinvented* recipes to accommodate a diet with low-sodium, including infusing them with unique, creative elements that elevate them beyond a simple list of ingredients and instructions. The recipes in this book are protected by the specific ways they are expressed. A set of ingredients, the ratio for their inclusion, a basic cooking method, and a standard recipe layout are un-protectable ideas. The recipes include personal effort and stories and thoughts. This is our Ménière's Low-Sodium Cookbook.

If you spot an error, let us know so we can correct it. *lillypillypublishing@outlook.com*

ISBN: paperback print: 978-1-7643118-9-2
      hardcopy print: 978-0-9943982-7-7
      eBook: 978-0-9943982-5-3

Cover design by Lilly Pilly Publishing
Cover image by Adobe Stock
Interior images by Adobe Stock & 123RF

No AI has been used in the creation of this book.

In 2023, Sally Edsall reached out to Julieann Wallace asking if we could create a low-sodium cookbook for Ménière's disease. It wouldn't be until 2025 that we would accomplish this. An enormous thank you to Sally Edsall, Kim Dean, Anne Elias, Phillip Stephanou, and Julieann Wallace, for their support of this cookbook.

Dedicated to those who have *Ménière's disease*, in response to the many who ask, 'Does anyone have any good recipes with low sodium?'

Ménière's disease is a chronic inner ear disorder causing unpredictable, disabling episodes of vertigo (spinning), fluctuating hearing loss, deafness, tinnitus (ringing in the ear), and a feeling of ear fullness. Researchers believe Ménière's is caused by genetics, inflammatory response (to head trauma, viruses, bacterial infections, auto-immune inner ear disease, systemic inflammation) or noise-induced (*Professor Jose Antonio Lopez Escamez, Associate Professor Dr Daniel Brown*, et al). The worst debilitating symptom, vertigo, is linked to either an abnormal buildup of fluid in the inner ear, or inflammation. Treatments focus on managing symptoms with medications, lifestyle changes like a low-salt diet, or, in severe cases, middle ear injections or surgery.

While there is an endless amount of low-sodium recipes available online today, the recipes in this cookbook come from members of the Ménière's community, *in the hope that they help you.*

Profits from sales will be donated to Ménière's research to help find a cure, or treatments that will lead to a return to a high quality of lived life.

Meet the Team

Sally Edsall a keen home cook, with a collection of recipes dating back to the 1980s. She developed Ménière's in 2016, and has been on a low-sodium cook since then. While she misses the concept of Vegemite on toast, she doesn't miss the actual taste of salt! Since diagnosis, Sally and her husband have continued their love of travelling, and are familiar with supermarkets and fresh food markets in lots of places around the world. This not only means a low-sodium diet is maintained, but it's a great way to mingle with locals away from the tourist beat.

Kim and Paul Dean are proud to own *Low Sodium Foods Australia*, taking over the business from the previous owners in 2021. Kim was diagnosed with Ménière's disease in 2010, and that is when she began her journey adopting a low salt diet, eating only foods containing no more sodium than 120mg per 100g. Their online store takes the struggle out of the search for low-sodium foods, especially the pantry basics. They love nothing more than helping everyone on their low-sodium journey and lifestyle.

Anne Elias was diagnosed with Ménière's in 2015. She had no idea what Ménière's disease was then, but soon learnt, and decided to start a support group that same year. The Sydney Ménière's Support has been a wonderful success. Anne is also the instigator of Zoom Webinars for Ménière's disease. For each of the Webinars, she invites professionals from the area of Ménière's disease to give positive sources of information and crucial connections. Anne has a cochlear implant, and is a *Ménière's Research Australia Ambassador*.

Phillip Stephanou was diagnosed with Ménière's disease after years of unpredictable symptoms and silent battles. With a deep passion for mindset, wellness, and resilience, he decided to turn his struggle into a source of strength for others. Phillip founded *Steady Through the Storm* - a platform dedicated to empowering people living with chronic illness through powerful storytelling, stoic mindset tools, and daily encouragement. His mission is simple but strong: *to help others keep moving forward, even in the face of life's loudest storms.*

Julieann Wallace was diagnosed with Ménière's in 1995. In 2020 she received a cochlear implant. She is the author of a bestselling novel with a Ménière's character, 'The Colour of Broken' (Amelia Grace), twice longlisted to be made into a movie, #1 on Amazon numerous times, and the sequel, 'All the Colours Above'. She has penned the books below, donating 100% of profits from sales to Ménière's research to help find a cure/treatments. Julieann is also a secondary teacher, artist, chocoholic, tea ninja, and tries not to scare her dog & cat away with her terrible cello playing. She is a *Ménière's Research Australia Ambassador* & *Cochlear Implant Buddy for Cochlear Australia*.

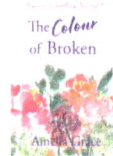       

Eat less from the box,
more from the earth.

Cooking fail?
Nailed it!

In a world full of trends,
a home-cooked meal remains a classic.

When you mix good flavors,
then the food turns into an orchestra.

I make salt disappear.

What's your superpower?

Good to Know!

Here's some information that you may find important, or just good to know, or refreshens your memory. And sometimes it's that boost you need to help you to start again to slay the Ménière's beast.

Ménière's Disease & Salt	i
Salt vs Sodium	ii
Sugar Alternatives	iii
Salt Substitutes	iv
Foods that Fight Inflammation	v
The Art of Salt Flavour - without the salt	vi
Grab & Go	vii
Panic! I've had too much salt/sodium	viii
Measurement Conversion Page	xviii
4 Week Meal Plan	163
My 4 Week Meal Plan	168
Nutrition & Exercise	173
My Exercise Plan	180
Index of Recipes	182

 ## Mindset & Gratitude

Your *mindset* sets your day. The *moment* you wake up *name 3 things* you are *thankful* for. *Every. Single. Day.*

Having the most terriblest, worstest, sh*%tiest of a day? Take a breath. *Think* - it's a new moment now! And don't stay stuck in the moment - think *what's next?*

Recipes

While there are hundreds of thousands of low-sodium recipes that have been published, the following recipes are tried and true by people with Ménière's, passed down through families, created, written from memories, and stumbled upon in the chaos of cooking. Thank you to the many dizzy cooks, named and unnamed, who have shared their favourite Ménière's foods and recipes, so we can help each other and raise money to donate to Ménière's research.

Chicken Seasoning & Rubs	ix
Beef, Pork, Lamb Seasonings & Rubs	xi
Seafood Seasonings	xiii
Vegetable Seasonings	xiv
This Goes with That…	xv
Breakfast	1
That Morning Liquid…	9
Drinks Throughout the Day	14
Lunch	17
My Lunches	38
Feeling Snackish	41
My Go to Snacks	52
Dinner	55
My Dinners	104
Mmm … Dessert	107
My Desserts	116
Party Food	119
My Party Food	126
BBQ	129
- BBQ Rubs & Marinades	130
- Salad Dressings	134
My BBQ food	136
Christmas	139
My Christmas Recipes	160
4 Week Eating Plan	163
My Food Planner	168
Nutrition & Exercise	173
My Exercise Plan	180

Ménière's Disease & Salt

For *many* (but not all) people with Ménière's disease, **salt is an enemy**. *One of the theories* about causes of Ménière's symptoms, is that salt makes the body retain water, increasing fluid pressure in the ears, causing vertigo, hearing loss and tinnitus. And that's why a low salt diet is recommended - it helps reduce the fluid pressure in your inner ear, and can help control the debilitating symptoms of Ménière's disease. It's recommended that a total of 100mg to 1500mg of sodium per day is observed (½ to ¾ teaspoon, or 2.5g to 4g of salt).

As if living with Ménière's disease isn't bad enough, it also affects our food choices and flavours. One of the many things that Ménièrians complain about is missing the flavour of salt. But instead of getting stuck on what we can't have, let's change our mindset and think, 'what's next?'. And that's using herbs and spices to take our food in a whole new direction.

Become a Ménière's Food Ninja! Read labels on food packaging!

Food packaging lists the total sodium content on the Nutrition Information Panel, as well as other ingredients containing sodium in the ingredients list. Sodium is listed as *sodium*, but can also be represented by other terms like *salt, MSG,* or *baking soda*. The total sodium includes *naturally occurring sodium, added salt,* and s*odium from other additives*, so the Nutrition Information Panel provides the most accurate measure of total sodium for a serving. When looking at the ingredients listed on the food packaging, if salt or sodium is in the top three ingredients, the product is likely high in sodium.

Other forms of sodium: Be aware that sodium can appear under other names in the ingredients list, such as:

Baking soda, Disodium guanylate (GMP), Disodium inosinate (IMP), Fleur de sel, Himalayan pink salt, Kosher salt, Monosodium glutamate (MSG), Monosodium glutamate (MSG), Rock salt, Sodium benzoate, Sodium bicarbonate, Sodium chloride, Sodium nitrate, Trisodium phosphate

Nutrient content claims: Look for claims such as "no added salt" or "reduced salt," but also double-check the sodium content on the Nutrition Information Panel, as these foods can still be high in sodium.

A warning about too little sodium in your diet

Sometimes, people on a low-salt diet **restrict their sodium too much**. This leads to a condition called *hyponatremia*, and causes symptoms like muscle cramps, fatigue, nausea, vomiting and headaches. If left untreated, it will worsen and result in confusion, seizures, coma and even death - though severe deficiency is uncommon.

Salt vs Sodium

Many people think salt and sodium are the same things. But they're not.

- *Sodium is what's found in food*, and occurs in nearly all *natural* foods, but especially in processed food containing preservatives, enhancing colour or adding texture. Sodium is an essential mineral and chemical element vital for nerve and muscle function and maintaining the body's fluid balance.
- *Salt is what we add to our food.* It adds flavour to food and is used as a binder and stabilizer. Salt, also known as sodium chloride (NaCl), is about 40% *sodium* and 60% *chloride*, so it's a chemical compound. And fact, it's the *sodium* that is detrimental to health. Consequently, it's the chloride of the chemical compound that gives food that "salty" taste.

Sodium - Most foods you eat contain sodium, though whole foods like vegetables, fruits and poultry contain much lower amounts. Plant-based foods like fresh produce generally have less sodium than animal-based foods, such as meat and dairy products. Sodium is most concentrated in processed and packaged foods like chips, frozen dinners and fast food where salt is added during processing to enhance flavor. Another major contributor to sodium intake is adding salt to food when preparing meals in your kitchen and as a seasoning before eating.

The Importance of Chloride

Chloride is a mineral *naturally* found in foods and our main food source is through sodium chloride, aka, salt. It's an electrolyte, meaning it carries an electric charge, along with sodium and potassium. Chloride helps regulate the amount of fluid and types of nutrients going in and out of our cells, and *plays a crucial role in maintaining fluid balance, regulating acid-base levels in the body, enabling nerve and muscle cell function.* It maintains our pH levels, stimulates stomach acid for digestion and the action of nerve and muscle cells, and facilitates the flow of oxygen and carbon dioxide within cells.

The Importance of Potassium

If you're managing salt content in your diet, it's helpful to also focus on adding in higher potassium foods too! *Potassium lessens the effects of sodium!* These are some go to foods high in potassium -
Fruit (mangoes, watermelon, dried apricots, pomegranate, avocado, banana, oranges, rockmelon, honeydew melon, guava, kiwi fruit, dates just to name a few), vegetables (potatoes, butternut squash, sweet potatoes, yams, tomatoes, silverbeet, beetroot, dark leafy greens - spinach, broccoli, cucumbers, pumpkin, zucchini, eggplant, beans, lentils, chickpeas, peas, unsalted nuts, cashews, almonds, to name a few), Greek yogurt, coconut water, fish - cod, salmon, canned tuna (check sodium content), beef, chicken, pork, chocolate, dairy and plant milks.

Sugar Alternatives

About Sugar

While sugar isn't inherently bad, it's necessary: Our bodies run on sugar. It's a simple *carbohydrate* that is produced naturally in all plants, including fruits, vegetables and even nuts. Carbohydrates are the preferred energy source for the body because the majority provide glucose. *Glucose is the fuel your brain, organs and muscles need to function and engage in everyday activities.* It's important to remember that sugar and other carbohydrates are found in foods that are important for your health in fruit, vegetables, milk, grains and legumes. Without these foods in your diet, you may be at risk of energy and nutritional deficiency.

For some people with Ménière's disease, sugar is a trigger for their symptoms. Hopefully these sugar substitutes will help with food preparation if that is you.

Applesauce - 1 cup of applesauce = 1 cup of sugar, but reduce other liquids in recipe.
Dates - 1 cup of date paste = 1 cup of sugar.
Fruit puree - ½ to 1 cup of fruit puree = 1 cup of sugar
Honey - ¾ cup of honey = 1 cup of sugar
Maple syrup - ¾ cup of maple syrup = 1 cup of sugar
Mashed banana - ½ cup of mashed banana = 1 cup of sugar generally
Molasses - 1 cup of molasses = 1 cup of sugar, but reduce other liquids in the recipe.
Stevia (derived from natural sources) 1 teaspoon = 1 cup of sugar

Naturally occurring sugars: lactose in milk, fructose in fruit and honey, glucose in fruits and vegetables, maltose in wheat and barley. They also have useful nutrients like fibre and vitamins and minerals.

Added sugars are sugars added to food by a manufacturer to make food taste sweeter, extend its shelf life, or improve its appearance. *They are also low in vitamins and minerals and high in kilojoules.* Sugars may be listed on labels under different names, such as: sucrose, glucose, dextrose maltose, golden syrup, maple syrup, molasses, coconut sugar, agave syrup, high-fructose corn syrup.

Artificial Sweeteners are created from chemicals in a lab. Some experts believe that artificial sweeteners pose health hazards, from weight gain to cancer. Be sure to do some research.

Salt Substitutes

People with Ménière's prepare their food without salt to circumnavigate a vertigo attack. But still, it's nice to have flavours in our cuisine. *Let's make our food flavoursome again!*

Apple cider vinegar - sweet and tart

Balsamic vinegar - sharp tart, hint of sweetness

Basil - sweet, savoury, peppery, notes of mint and anise

Cardamom - citrusy, sweet, notes of ginger, cinnamon and clove

Cinnamon - slightly sweet and peppery undertones

Coconut aminos - tastes like soy sauce with a hint of sweetness.

Coriander - warm, floral, lemony taste

Cumin - nutty, bitter, pungent, hint of citrus

Dill - hints of celery and fennel

Dried onion or onion powder - adds a flavour boost to savoury recipes

Garlic - add to marinades, tomato sauces, stir-fries and soups

Ginger - pungent, sweet bite

Ground black pepper - may also decrease inflammation

Lemon juice - acidity brings out flavours

Mint - cool and refreshing

Nutritional yeast - adds a cheesy, savoury flavour

Oregano - strong, pungent flavour that's warm, earthy, and slightly bitter, with notes of camphor, mint, and a hint of pepper and sweetness

Rosemary - piney, woody, and pungent, with complex notes of evergreen, citrus, mint, and peppery undertones

Red pepper flakes - earthy, slightly smoky, and sometimes mildly fruity or floral notes

Saffron - sweet, floral, and earthy with notes of honey, hay, and a subtle hint of metallic bitterness

Sage - earthy, pungent, and piney, with warm, slightly bitter, and fresh notes of eucalyptus and mint, sometimes with hints of citrus and vanilla

Seaweed powder - umami, a rich, savory, and delicious taste, with a distinct briny and oceanic flavour that can also have subtle smoky or mushroom-like notes

Smoked paprika - woody, earthy, savory, and slightly sweet, with a dominant smoky flavour

Tarragon - sweet licorice-like, grassy, fresh, slightly bitter with touches of vanilla, mint, pepper, and eucalyptus

Thyme - strong, earthy flavour, similar to rosemary or lavender

Truffle oil - earthy, mushroomy, and garlicky

Turmeric - earthy, warm, and slightly bitter taste with musky, peppery, and ginger-like undertones

Heart Salt - contains 56% less sodium than ordinary salt and is MSG free .
nepbio.com.au/products/heartsalt-table-salt400gr

Foods that Fight Inflammation

Ménière's is a group of rare symptoms (disorders) of the inner ear – recurring episodic vertigo (Ménière's disease researcher, *Associate Professor Dr Daniel Brown* (Curtin University, Australia) calls it the "Dizzy Terror"), sensorineural hearing loss, and roaring tinnitus, plus a feeling of ear fullness or pressure in the ear. The difficulty in finding a one stop cure or treatment that helps all people with Ménière's, is that research has shown it is caused by multiple factors – Researchers believe Ménière's is caused by genetics, inflammatory response, and noise induced. So if you ever hear of someone who has one treatment that will help everyone, be aware that it won't.

According to *Professor Jose Antonio Lopez Escamez*, Head of Ménière disease Neuroscience Laboratory, Kolling Institute, University of Sydney, Australia, "Chronic systemic inflammation is observed in 60% of patients with MD that could be confirmed measuring cytokines in plasma. The patients with no inflammation (40%) are likely to be a genetic condition, even without familial history, since most are recessive disorders." He also said, "Other subgroups of Ménière's disease patients have migraine or an autoimmune disorder, including autoimmune thyroid disease or rheumatoid arthritis which requires a multi-disciplinary approach to control the symptoms."

Our food intake affects every part of our body, and influences our state of mind. The problem with commercial food is that it is highly processed or ultra-processed, and has many added ingredients such as sugar, salt, fat, and artificial colors or preservatives. Ultra-processed foods are made mostly from substances extracted from foods - fats, starches, added sugars, hydrogenated fats. They may also contain additives like artificial colours and flavours or stabilizers. *This leads to chronic inflammation.*

With that in mind, consider an eating plan of anti-inflammatory foods, and keep a food diary. While there isn't one specific anti-inflammatory diet, experts say overall healthy eating patterns can help you get rid of inflammation and stay healthier. In particular, they recommend the foods to the left can help bring inflammation down, as well as gut-healthy foods. The Mediterranean diet may be the most beneficial in helping with inflammation.

Benefits include improved joint and muscle pain, better gut and brain health, improved mood, healthier overall due to increased nutrient intake from foods rich in antioxidants, vitamins, minerals, and healthy fats.

The Art of Salt Flavour without the Salt

Options to Make Your Food Pop!

- Vinegar: balsamic, red wine vinegar, apple cider vinegars add a tart and complex flavour
- Citrus: fresh lime and lemon juices add a bright 'bite' to your food similar to salt
- Salt Substitutes: e.g. NoSalt, Heart Salt, Fitsalt, Nu-Salt etc, taste similar to salt, but should be used with caution if you have kidney disease or failure
- Ground black pepper is the closest to salt in flavour
- Fresh garlic or ginger
- Infused oils (garlic or chilli oil)
- Fresh or dried herbs - rosemary, oregano, basil, parsley, dill or spices - paprika, turmeric, white mustard, chilli flakes

All Purpose Seasoning

This combination is widely used by many people seeking a salty-ish flavour without salt.

- black pepper - ¼ teaspoon
- dried onion powder and garlic powder - 2 tablespoons each
- dried thyme - 1½ teaspoons
- paprika - 1 tablespoon

Combine and store in an airtight container or shaker jar.

Add Your Own Salt Replacement Go -To Combinations (do some research)

_____
_____
_____
_____
_____
_____

A reminder about restricting sodium too much - Not getting enough sodium may cause issues, *like increasing resistance to insulin and raising LDL cholesterol levels*. Sodium is an important electrolyte and the main component of table salt. *Too much sodium* has been linked to *high blood pressure*, and health organizations recommend limiting your intake *(healthline.com/nutrition/6-dangers-of-sodium-restriction)*.

Grab and Go,
and for an *accidental high-sodium intake*

Low-Sodium, High-Potassium Foods

In a hurry to leave? Here's a quick hit list of foods to grab, and, always have water with you. An added bonus with this list is that, if you've had too much salt, these foods and liquids will help flush out the excess sodium from your body, and hopefully reduce the chances of a vertigo attack. *Already out and about?* These foods and products are always available in stores.

- banana
- avocado
- kiwi fruit
- mango
- watermelon
- dried apricots
- oranges
- rockmelon
- honeydew melon
- guava
- dates
- apple
- unsalted nuts
- cashews
- almonds
- water
- milk
- plain yogurt (add your own fruit) - helps your gut and digestive system function at its best
- coconut water - also contains electrolytes like magnesium and calcium that help balance fluid levels.
- ginger tea
- peppermint tea (helps your body digest fatty food)

Note: drinking too much water, hyponatremia, can cause low blood sodium (headache, brainfog, confusion, lethargy, nausea, vomiting, seizures, coma and even death).

Consistent and adequate fluid intake, distributed evenly throughout the day, may help reduce vertigo and hearing symptoms. Your fluid intake will also vary due to weather and exercise. 6 - 8 cups of fluid a day is a general guide.

Panic!
I've had too much salt/sodium!

Get moving and sweat!

It will help your body get rid of the excess sodium.
Be sure that your exercise is safe for your balance,
and within your limits.

And the *Grab and Go* foods will also help
flush out the excess sodium from your body,
plus water, milk, coconut water, ginger or peppermint tea!

And of course we ALL do ballet!
That spinning... a pirouette!

Chicken Seasonings & Rubs

"Variety's the very spice of life, That gives it all its flavour" - English poet *William Cowper* (1785). We love to give variety to our meats for new tastes. Here's homemade seasonings and rubs to sprinkle over chicken prior to baking or grilling. No filler, free-flow agents, or additives, starches, or MSG, like in some commercial spice blends. Add for coating your chicken for deliciousness. Blend the seasonings to your liking, and store in a sealed jar. They will last for up to 6 months.

Chicken Spice Rub
2 teaspoons smoked paprika, 1 teaspoon onion powder, 1 teaspoon thyme (ground or dried), 1½ teaspoon black pepper, ½ teaspoon cayenne pepper, ½ teaspoon garlic powder

Chicken Spice Rub
1 teaspoon ground black pepper, 1 ½teaspoons dried parsley, 1 tablespoon garlic powder, 1½ teaspoons dried basil, 1 teaspoon ground mace, 1¼ teaspoons ground thyme, 1¼ teaspoons dried all purpose seasoning, 1 teaspoon dried sage, 1 teaspoon onion powder, ¼ teaspoon cayenne pepper

Italian Chicken Seasoning Mix
½ tablespoon rosemary, 1 tablespoon dried parsley, 2 tablespoons oregano, 1 tablespoon basil, 1 tablespoon thyme, ½ tablespoon marjoram

Smoky, Spicy, a little Sweet
2 tablespoons garlic powder, 2 tablespoons brown sugar, 1 tablespoon onion powder, 1 teaspoon thyme, 1 teaspoon smoked paprika, 1 teaspoon chilli powder, ½ teaspoon cayenne pepper or red pepper flakes, ½ teaspoon black pepper

Chicken All Purpose Seasoning
1 tablespoon garlic powder, 1½ teaspoons dried basil, 1½ teaspoons dried parsley, ¼ teaspoon dried savory, 1¼ teaspoons ground thyme, 1 teaspoon ground mace, 1 teaspoon onion powder, 1 teaspoon ground black pepper, 1 teaspoon dried sage, ¼ teaspoon cayenne pepper

Smoked Paprika Chicken Rub
Place your chicken thighs or breast in a bowl and cover it with this spice rub - 1 tablespoon smoked paprika, ½ teaspoon each ground cumin, garlic powder, and onion powder ¼ teaspoon cayenne pepper, 2 tablespoons olive oil. Let it sit for up to an hour before cooking in a pan - *add some lime wedges on the side.*

Greek Seasoning Mix
1 tablespoon basil, 2 teaspoons dill, 2 teaspoons garlic powder, 2 teaspoons onion powder, 1 tablespoon oregano, 2 teaspoons parsley, 1 teaspoon rosemary, 1 teaspoon thyme, 1 teaspoon ground black pepper

Spicy Chicken Rub
Low Sodium Foods Australia - fennel, oregano, paprika, garlic, onion powder, sumac, cumin, parsley, coriander and nutmeg, black pepper

Chicken Seasoning with Ground Mustard
2 tablespoons paprika, 2 tablespoons garlic powder, 2 teaspoons onion powder, 1 tablespoon ground mustard, 1 teaspoon cumin, 2-3 teaspoons cayenne pepper

French Onion Blend
4 tablespoons dried onion flakes, 2 tablespoons no-salt added beef bouillon, 1 teaspoon onion powder, 1 teaspoon garlic powder, 1 teaspoon dried parsley, ¼ teaspoon black pepper (use for dips or soups)

Cajun Blend
1 tablespoon oregano, 1 tablespoon paprika, 1 tablespoon cayenne pepper, 1 tablespoon black pepper, 1 teaspoon onion powder, 1 teaspoon garlic powder.

Homemade Curry Powder
85g coriander powder, 75g turmeric powder, 30g mustard seeds whole, 12g chilli powder, 6g ginger powder *the ground seed mixture*, 6g cumin seeds whole, 6g fenugreek seed whole. Grind mustard, cumin and fenugreek seeds to a fine powder. Combine the ground seed mixture with the remaining spices in a bowl, mix thoroughly to combine. Store in a tight sealed storage jar for up to a month.

Beef, Pork & Lamb Seasonings & Rubs

"Food is our common ground, a universal experience." - *James Beard*. Sometimes you just need a change up of flavours for your meat. Here's some homemade seasonings and rubs to use prior to baking or grilling. Blend the seasonings and store in a sealed jar. They will last for up to 6 months. Play with the flavours to suit.

Cajun Blend
1 tablespoon oregano, 1 tablespoon paprika, 1 tablespoon cayenne pepper, 1 tablespoon black pepper, 1 teaspoon onion powder, 1 teaspoon garlic powder

Chilli Seasoning
¾ cup chilli powder, 2 tablespoons ground cumin, 2 tablespoons dried oregano, 2 tablespoons minced onion, 2 tablespoons minced garlic (use 2 tablespoons of mix for 450g mince)

Italian Seasoning Blend
1 tablespoon basil, ½ tablespoon oregano, 1 tablespoon rosemary, 1 tablespoon parsley, ½ tablespoon onion powder, ½ tablespoon garlic powder

Mediterranean Blend
1 tablespoon garlic powder, 1 tablespoon onion powder, 1 tablespoon cumin, 2 tablespoons coriander, ½ tablespoon cayenne, 2 tablespoons oregano, 1 tablespoon thyme

Ranch Salad Blend
2½ tablespoons parsley, 2 teaspoons dried dill, 2½ teaspoons garlic powder, 2½ teaspoons onion powder, 2 teaspoons dried minced onion, 1 teaspoon black pepper

Seasoned Blend
1 tablespoon onion powder, ½ teaspoon garlic powder, 1½ teaspoons ground celery seed, ½ teaspoon paprika, ½ teaspoon chilli powder, ¼ teaspoon cayenne (optional)

Spice Blend Recipe
1½ tablespoons onion powder, 1 tablespoon garlic powder, 1 tablespoon paprika, 1 tablespoon dry mustard, ½ tablespoon crushed thyme leaves, ½ teaspoon white pepper, ¼ teaspoon celery seed

Taco Seasoning
¼ cup chilli powder, 2 teaspoons paprika, 1 teaspoon garlic powder, 2 tablespoons ground cumin, 1 teaspoon onion powder, 1 teaspoon dried oregano (use 2 tablespoons for 450g mince)

Beefy Blend with Mustard
5 teaspoons onion powder, 1 tablespoon garlic powder, 1 tablespoon paprika, 1 tablespoon ground mustard, 1 teaspoon dried thyme, ½ teaspoon pepper, ½ teaspoon celery seed

Curry Powder Alternative
1 teaspoon of ground ginger, ¼ teaspoon of chilli powder ~ *Greg*. You can also add 3 tablespoons turmeric, 3 tablespoons coriander, 3 tablespoons cumin and 1 tablespoon black pepper

Flavoursome Steak & Veggie Seasoning
2 tablespoons black pepper, 2 tablespoons garlic powder, 1 tablespoon smoked paprika, 1 tablespoon onion powder, 1 teaspoon dried thyme, 1 teaspoon dried rosemary, 1 teaspoon ground cumin

Steakhouse Spice Rub
2 teaspoons brown sugar, 2 teaspoons onion powder, 1 teaspoon black pepper, freshly ground, 2 teaspoons garlic powder

BBQ Steak Rub
Low Sodium Foods Australia - wattle seed, paprika, parsley, cumin, coriander, onion powder, garlic powder, ginger, fennel, cinnamon, paprika, sumac, black pepper, and crushed chilli flakes

Pork Rub
Low Sodium Foods Australia - allspice, oregano, cumin, coriander, sweet paprika, smoked paprika, fennel, sumac, cinnamon, garlic, onion, thyme, black pepper

Lamb Rub
3 teaspoons garlic powder, 2 teaspoons ground coriander, 2 teaspoons ground cumin, 2 teaspoons sweet paprika, ¼ teaspoon ground cloves, pinch of cinnamon, pinch of cardamom

Lamb Dry Spice Rub
1 teaspoon paprika, 1½ teaspoons dried thyme, 1½ teaspoons dried basil, ¾ teaspoon cumin, 2 tablespoons curry powder

Seafood Seasonings

"A recipe has no soul. You, as the cook, must *bring soul* to the recipe." - *Thomas Keller*. Here's some homemade seasonings and rubs to use prior to baking or grilling with seafood. Blend the seasonings and store in a sealed jar. Play with the flavours to suit. They will last for up to 6 months.

Fish Blend
2 tablespoons paprika, 2–3 teaspoons cayenne pepper, 2 tablespoons garlic powder, 2 teaspoons onion powder, 1 tablespoons dry mustard, 1 teaspoon cumin

Lemon & Garlic
A squeeze of lemon and chopped garlic. Lime, lemon, grapefruit or orange is always a fresh flavor.

Teriyaki Sauce
2 tablespoons cornstarch + ¼ cup of water (mix and set aside). In a pot over medium to high heat add 1 cup of water, ¼ cup reduced-sodium soy sauce, ¼ cup honey, 1 garlic clove, ½ teaspoon of fresh chopped ginger - as it begins to bubble, add cornstarch and stir until the mixture thickens.

Honey Mustard Sauce
½ cup whole grain mustard, ¼ cup extra-virgin olive oil, ¼ cup of honey, 2 cloves of garlic, minced fine, ½ teaspoon red pepper flakes

Herbs
Herb rubs are amazing with light tasting fish - parsley, dill, cilantro, thyme, oregano, and mint

Mango Salsa
1 ripe mango, diced, 1 red pepper, finely chopped, ½ red onion, diced, 1 jalapeno, minced, 1 tablespoon cilantro, juice of 1 lime - mix and serve over fish of your choice.

Cajun Fish Seasoning
3 tablespoons smoked paprika, 2 tablespoons garlic powder, 1 tablespoon ground black pepper, 1 tablespoons onion powder, 1 tablespoon dried thyme, 1 tablespoon dried oregano, ½ tablespoon cayenne, ½ tablespoon crushed red pepper - keeps for up to 6 months

Crab, Shrimp, Oyster Seasoning
2 teaspoons ground bay leaves, 3½ teaspoons celery seed, 1 tablespoon sweet paprika, 1 teaspoon dry mustard powder, ½ teaspoon ground ginger, ½ teaspoon ground black pepper, ¼ teaspoon ground nutmeg, ¼ teaspoon ground cinnamon, ¼ teaspoon cayenne, ⅛ teaspoon ground, allspice, ⅛ teaspoon ground cloves, ⅛ teaspoon cardamom (optional)

Vegetable Seasonings

Savoury Spice Blend
2 tablespoons nutritional yeast, 1 tablespoon onion powder, 2 teaspoons garlic powder, 1 tablespoon dried parsley, 1 tablespoon dried basil, 2 teaspoons dried thyme, 2 teaspoons mustard powder, 2 teaspoons paprika, ½ teaspoon ground turmeric, ½ teaspoon celery seeds

Roast Veggie Seasoning Recipe
1 tablespoon garlic powder, 2 teaspoons dried oregano, 2 teaspoons onion powder, 1½ teaspoons smoked paprika, 1 teaspoon dried basil, 1 teaspoon ground black pepper

Roasted Vegetable Seasoning
1 tablespoon garlic granules, ½ tablespoon onion powder, 1½ tablespoons paprika (smoked and sweet paprika), ½ tablespoon parsley, 1 teaspoon dried rosemary, ½ tablespoon thyme, 1 teaspoon black pepper. Toss veggies in oil before adding the seasoning then baking.

Vegetable Taco Seasoning Mix
4 tablespoons chilli powder, 2 tablespoons paprika, 1 tablespoon garlic powder, 1 tablespoon onion powder, 1 tablespoon black pepper, 1 tablespoon cumin, 1 tablespoon crushed red pepper, 1 tablespoon cornstarch

Simply
olive oil, fresh cracked ground pepper, fresh rosemary to taste

Italian Seasoning
4 tablespoons dried basil, 2 tablespoons dried oregano, 2 tablespoons dried rosemary, 2 tablespoons dried marjoram, 2 tablespoons dried thyme, 2 tablespoons red pepper flakes

This Goes With That...

"Bees do have a smell, you know, and if they don't they should, for their feet are dusted with spices from a million flowers." ~ Ray Bradbury. The following is just a general guide for the art of flavour without salt. Be sure to look up specifics of cultural blends for the overall taste sensation you are pursuing. Don't blend them altogether at once. Fine tune to your taste preferences.

Beef
basil, bay leaf, caraway, cayenne, chilli, cumin, curry, dill, fenugreek, garlic, ginger, marjoram, mustard, oregano, paprika, parsley, rosemary, sage, savory, tarragon, thyme.

Chicken
allspice, anise, basil, bay leaf, borage, cayenne, chives, cinnamon, curry, dill, fenugreek, garlic, ginger, lemon, lovage, marjoram, mustard, nutmeg, onion, oregano, paprika, parsley, pepper, pesto, rosemary, sage, savory, tarragon, thyme.

Fish
allspice, anise, basil, bay leaf, borage, carraway, chervil, cayenne, chilli flakes, chives, coriander, cumin, curry, dill, fennel, garlic, ginger, lemon myrtle, marjoram, mustard, nutmeg, oregano, paprika, parsley, pesto, rosemary, saffron, sage, savory, tarragon, thyme, turmeric.

Fruit
allspice, anise, cinnamon, cloves, curry, ginger, mace, mint, nutmeg, pepper.

Lamb
basil, bay leaf, cardamom, cinnamon, coriander, cumin, curry, dill, garlic, ginger, lemon balm, mace, marjoram, mint, onion, oregano, paprika, parsley, rosemary, saffron, sage, tarragon, thyme, turmeric.

Pork
allspice, basil, cardamom, cloves, curry, garlic, ginger, marjoram, mustard, oregano, paprika, parsley, mustard, rosemary, sage, savory, thyme.

Turkey
basil, garlic, marjoram, onion, oregano, rosemary, saffron, sage, savory, tarragon, thyme

Vegetables
allspice, basil, cajun, cardamom, chilli flakes, garlic, ginger, marjoram, mint, parsley, pepper, oregano, thyme, rosemary, sage, thyme.

Some Spice & Herb Combinations to Explore

Beef
(lemon juice, rosemary, black pepper) - (thyme, cloves, orange peel, black pepper) - (garlic, herbed vinegar, black pepper) - (mashed green peppercorns, onions, marjoram) - (rosemary, thyme, oregano, sage, bay leaves) - (basil, rosemary, sage, thyme, and parsley)

Chicken
(ginger, orange peel, sage) - (rosemary, lemon zest, garlic) - (marjoram, thyme, apple cider vinegar) - (tarragon, shallots, lemon juice) - (basil, white wine vinegar, garlic) - (thyme, rosemary, oregano)

Fish
(dill, lemon juice, mustard seeds) - (basil, tarragon, dill, parsley) - (lovage, celery seeds, lemon juice, black pepper) - (fennel seeds, mustard seeds, bay, lemon peel) - (lemon zest, thyme, parsley, dill). *Research the different blends for different types of fish.*

Lamb
(oregano, parsley, rosemary, thyme) - (rosemary, garlic, mint) - (rosemary, garlic) - (mint, cumin, coriander, cinnamon) - (thyme, dijon mustard, lemon juice, honey)

Pork
(caraway, coriander, garlic, parsley, thyme) - (clove, cinnamon, coriander, curry, fennel, ginger, nutmeg) - (garlic, parsley, rosemary, sage, thyme) - (turmeric, cumin, rosemary)

Turkey
(garlic, lemon, onion, orange, rosemary, thyme) - (sage, thyme, black pepper, marjoram, rosemary, nutmeg)

Roasted Vegetables
(cajun, chilli, garlic, rosemary, thyme) - (olive oil, sage, thyme, rosemary)

www.lowsodiumfoods.com.au

Dedicated to serving people who rely on a diet that is low sodium,
with a friendly and efficient service, making your low-sodium journey easier.
Delivering internationally

Proudly owned by
Kim (diagnosed with Ménière's disease in 2010) & Paul Dean

- Beans
- Biscuits
- Bread products & cereal
- Cake mixes, Bread Mixes & Pancake Mixes
- Ceres organics
- Chef's choice couscous
- Chilli harvest
- Condiments & sauces
- Fish, chicken, beef
- Gift cards
- Gluten free
- Heartful flavours
- Herbies spices
- Hillfarm tasmania
- Honest to goodness
- Kangaroo island
- Lasting harvest dip mixes
- Liquid stock, powders & powders
- Maleny Cuisine
- Matzo crackers
- Meal Bases
- New england larder
- New products
- Orgran
- Pasta & noodles
- Pop's tomato sauce
- Quincy jones Jelly
- Red kelly salad dressings
- Salad dressings
- Salt skip
- Saucy spice co
- Snacks
- Soup
- Specials
- Spice Road Spices
- Spices, Mixes & Blends
- Spoonfed
- The Stock Merchant Free Range Stock
- Yes you can (Gluten Free Cake Mixes, pancake Mixes)

new products added regularly

Shop online and take the struggle out of the search for low-sodium foods, especially the pantry basics.

125 Reviews

WOW! To be able to bake again - thank you! - Gail
Absolutely fantastic! - Susan
Really speedy delivery, I am so happy with the products I purchased.
Will continue to shop on this site - Dale
Amazing company and products - Natalia

Measurement Conversions Page – a guide

The Australian and NZ cup is 250mL, the standard metric cup. The U.S. cup is 240mL, close enough to do a cup to cup conversion, except in critical baking recipes. The U.K. cup is 225mL, enough of a difference to do conversion calculations in baking recipes - write changes on the pages.

Oven temperatures

Celsius (electric)	Celsius (fan forced)	Fahrenheit	Gas
120º C	100º C	250º F	1 very slow
150º C	130º C	300º F	2 slow
160º C	140º C	325º F	3 moderately slow
180º C	160º C	350º F	4 moderate
190º C	170º C	375º F	5 moderately hot
200º C	180º C	400º F	6 hot
230º C	210º C	450º F	7 very hot
250º C	230º C	500º F	9 very hot

A fan-forced oven cooking time may be less.

Metric cup & spoon sizes

Cup	Metric
¼ cup	60mL
⅓ cup	80mL
½ cup	125mL
1 cup	250mL

Spoon	Metric
¼ teaspoon	1.25mL
½ teaspoon	2.5mL
1 teaspoon	5mL
2 teaspoons	10mL
1 tablespoon	20mL

Liquids

Metric	Cup
30mL	
60mL	¼ cup
80mL	⅓ cup
100mL	
125mL	½ cup
150mL	
180mL	¾ cup
200mL	
250mL	1 cup
310mL	1¼ cups
375mL	1½ cups
430mL	1¾ cups
475mL	
500mL	2 cups
625mL	2½ cups
750mL	3 cups
1L	4 cups
1.25L	5 cups
1.5L	6 cups
2L	8 cups
2.5L	10 cups

Mass (weight)

Metric	Imperial
10g	¼ oz
15g	½ oz
30g	1 oz
60g	2 oz
90g	3 oz
125g	4 oz (¼lb)
155g	5 oz
185g	6 oz
220g	7 oz
250g	8 oz (½lb)
280g	9 oz
315g	10 oz
345g	11 oz
375g	12 oz
410g	13 oz
440g	14 oz
470g	15 oz
500g (½ kg)	16 oz (1lb)
750g	24 oz (1½lb)
1kg	32 oz (2lb)
1.5kg	48 oz (3lb)
2kg	64 oz (4lb)

Waiter: What meal would you like to order?

Me: I want something solid, you know, a food that won't trigger my Meniere's ... You know ... like low salt, no caffeine, no sugar, not processed, more ... healthy ...

Waiter delivers meal...

Meniere's Cure Recipe

Ingredients

- a drop of vertigo forever stop
- a sprinkle of never-ending perfect hearing
- a large smidgen of ear fullness clearer
- a spread of perfect balance
- a dollop of tinnitus remover
- an infusion of good friends
- a pinch salt like we've never had before
- a drizzle of brainfog eraser
- an echo of no more tears
- a blend of sunny skies
- a gallon of beaming smiles as we're freed from the Ménière's prison
- a dash of humour

Method

1. Spin everything together in a blender.
2. Swirl it and drink like Alice in Wonderland.
3. Dance like no one is looking, round and round.
4. Feel your heart bloom with a spiral of happiness.
5. Eat whatever you like without fear for the term of your natural life.
6. Enjoy your life again.

recipe by Jules, 2025

Breakfast

Breakfast

Self-care is a big one for Ménière's disease.
Looking after yourself with your food intake to reduce symptoms
goes a long way to leading a better quality of life.
Having meals that are evenly spaced out throughout
the day *may* help to stabilise the fluid levels in the inner ear.
We have to try everything, right!
Commercial breakfast cereals can hide a significant amount of salt, and sugar.
So ideally, *making your own breakfast* gives you
more control of the salt & sugar content.

Turning breakfast into an art form,
one bowl or plate masterpiece at a time.

Breakfast is the canvas
upon which you paint your day.

Feeling egg-straordinary
with my breakfast spread.

Breakfast...

I love porridge with added pumpkin and sunflower seeds, hemp protein powder (has zero sodium unlike all the pea based ones), pears (cooked in with the oats), and added frozen berries. Add cinnamon and ginger if desired. Also sub stewed rhubarb for pears. If desired top with honey or maple syrup.

Two gluten free Weet-Bix for me, mixed with warm water and protein powder of choice - press into a container - add yoghurt (coconut for me being DF/GF) - add berries and drizzle with choc sauce, maple syrup or cinnamon. Leave overnight and it sets like a soft cheesecake. Never been a Weet-Bix person! *But I love this!*

I have oats and then put walnuts or any nuts I have, sultanas, pumpkin seeds, linseed seeds in a little blender to make the seeds smaller and have it with the oats and fruits (love papaya, banana, blueberry and raspberries) yoghurt and low fat milk and a spoon of rosehip powder that is high in vitamin C so I don't get arthritis pain.

I like a chia pot - layers of chia seeds which I soak, yoghurt, and fresh berries or things like canned peaches. A few crushed walnuts or the like on top.

I have poached eggs with smashed avocado and cooked tomato.

Sometimes I have porridge with fruit and low fat milk and yoghurt.

I have honey yoghurt, unsalted nuts (walnuts, almonds, peanuts, macadamias and pistachios) most days. Other days I will have low-sodium bread (toasted) with no-added salt peanut butter.

I love to make my own cereal with oats, sultanas or cranberries, coconut flakes, chopped walnuts, almond flakes. Anything you like can be added.

Morning Sun untoasted muesli (low-sodium). I add LSA (linseed, sunflower seed and almond meal) and berries to the muesli, add milk and microwave it for one minute to improve the texture for me.

When I have the time, *usually on weekends*, I like to make blueberry pancakes using sodium-free baking powder.

I just love porridge with raspberries, blueberries, strawberries and chia seeds. It starts my day off right!

A small layer of Carman's plain toasted muesli, yoghurt, berries, another sprinkle of muesli. Juggling MD and diabetes!

I love buckwheat porridge, soak the while the night before and then cook in the morning with some fruit, psyllium husk and hemp seeds. And some lactose-free yogurt. Gluten and lactose-free, makes my tummy feel good and nice and warm on a cold morning.

Avocado on my homemade low-sodium bread with a squeeze of lemon juice and pepper on top.

Breakfast...

After my fill of porridge, oats etc, I've started experimenting with homemade pancakes of both the sweet and savoury variety. So either topped with berries and yoghurt and honey and cinnamon and chopped nuts etc or filled with grated zucchini or carrot and a splash of homemade or low salt tomato sauce for a bit of extra flavour. *Delicious.* I add oats to the pancake mix just to be good sometimes.

I don't eat breakfast. I practice intermittent fasting to reduce inflammation. I've found it's helped my MD symptoms.

A smoothie with soy milk, banana, strawberries, baby spinach, unsalted peanut butter, wheatgerm, flaxseed, turmeric, cardamom, cinnamon and finally nutmeg. *I also have* low-salt bread with my homemade jam.

In winter, good old scrambled eggs on top of some large mushrooms as a bread substitute.

I love a good açai bowl. Acai, fresh berries, banana and homemade granola.

Low sugar granola with added fruit, seeds, nuts with either yoghurt or almond milk.

Depending on how I am feeling, I go for a 30 minute walk, then have low-sodium toast with a peanut butter, honey and banana on top.

⅓ cup quick oats, mashed banana, 1 egg, dash cinnamon then a few blueberries. Mix in a mug and pop in the microwave for 2 minutes.

Homemade pork and fennel sausages, hash brown and low-salt baked beans. Mushroom, wilted kale and poached egg is a nice high protein brekky.

Pancakes. *Yum!* Eggs and avocado on toast. Add tomatoes. Greek yoghurt with honey and banana. Fruit. *I love* yoghurt, fresh (or frozen) berries, topped with muesli clusters.

Poached egg on avocado with cottage cheese. Good protein source for the morning. *Before I eat anything*, I drink warm water with grated ginger and lemon juice.

My go to is 2 scrambled eggs (just 2 fresh eggs with a dash of water or sometimes milk) with sauerkraut, but sometimes I mix it up with a date, cinnamon and ginger porridge.

I have porridge with fruit and low-fat milk and yoghurt.

I make my own muesli - uncooked wholemeal oats, a few walnuts, a few blueberries, sunflower seeds, pepitas, mixed together. Soak overnight with enough water to cover the oats. You can also use juice instead of water if you prefer. Serve with low-fat yoghurt and add slices banana. And a morning coffee!

Wholegrain vanilla oat porridge with berries & banana. Make the porridge. Add layer spoonfuls of porridge, berries & banana, on repeat. Drizzle with maple syrup.

Breakfast...

Acai bowl for me. Acai sorbet. Chopped up banana, blueberries, raspberries, kiwi fruit, slithered almonds, walnuts, pistachios and whatever else I want to throw on top. Yum! Except in winter. Then it's porridge with banana and honey on top.

On weekends, I love pancakes, topped with banana and strawberries and blueberries and a drizzle of maple syrup.

Weet-Bix and mango smoothie bowl is just ... *mmmm!* Blend 200g frozen mango, ⅓ cup of natural yoghurt, ⅓ cup almond milk, maple syrup to taste, all blended. Throw it into a bowl, top with 2 Weet-Bix, mango slices, blueberries, coconut flakes or sliced almonds.

Mini quiche bites *hit the spot -* saute diced onion and finely chopped red capsicum, then put in baby spinach until it wilts. Add to ½ cup cheese, ¼ milk and 4 eggs mixture. Bake for 25 minutes.

My partner makes me a low-salt burrito wrapped around scrambled egg and melted low-salt cheese. I add chilli jam sometimes. He has bacon just to annoy me!

SPC flakes. *They have a* protein that regulates fluid & ion in balance.

Homemade pancakes with whipped egg whites, maple syrup, blueberries.

My Breakfasts

That morning liquid...

In 2024, in a *randomised trial* of 50 patients, a low-sodium diet
with adequate *water intake* improved hearing and alleviated vertigo
and tinnitus in some Ménière's patients.
Worth a try if you haven't already increased your water intake.
ENTs recommend drinking adequate amounts of fluid daily.
That fluid should include water, milk, low sugar fruit juices
or carbonated soft drinks.
According to Menieres.org.uk, 'coffee, tea and alcohol can be a problem
as they cause the tiniest blood vessels at the very end of the system to contract
and so restrict the blood supply to the inner ear. *A cup or two is one thing*
but 10 or more strong coffees a day could make your symptoms much worse.
Small amounts of alcohol - half a pint of beer, a glass of red wine
or a pub measure of spirits - may actually *improve the peripheral circulation,*
but any more has the opposite effect.'

But as in all things, you choose what works best for your body.

Today's good mood is sponsored by ...
whatever your Meniere's tolerates for a morning liquid.

If this is coffee,
please bring me some tea;
but if this is tea,
please bring me something that won't put me in a spin.

You're brew-tiful.

That morning liquid...

Mmmm...a breakfast smoothie.

Decaf coffee. Decaf green tea. Decaf tea. Skinny chai latte - no caffeine at all.

Organic apple cider vinegar with honey lemon ginger cardamom tea.

Rooibos (Redbush) tea has no caffeine and can be drunk with milk if you prefer tea that way. It doesn't taste like black tea but it's got the same vibe as tea with milk. Apparently full of things that are good for you too!

At the moment...freshly squeezed blood orange juice. Oh, and decaf coffee with fluffy milk - made in my moka coffee pot and a milk frother! Or decaf *Twinings English Breakfast* tea. Or tasty rosehip and hibiscus tea. Depends on mood.

Hubby has a coffee machine. I use decaf coffee, a mini electric whisk to froth the coffee so it looks like a proper espresso. The coffee machine also has an automatic milk froth. I feel like I'm having a 'real' cafe latte treat!!

Decaf coffee espresso with MCT (medium-chain triglyceride) oil.

I'm a Milo girl on the weekends. During the week is usually a glass of pineapple juice with breakfast before rushing to work.

I'm the most boring coffee drinker as I don't like milk. So it's a decaf black coffee.

A decaf coffee...*I still want to feel 'normal'*, even though there's no glorious caffeine.

I drink a mixture I make with a lemon, orange, cracked black pepper, turmeric, ginger, honey, & coconut water. I have this all blended together. Then frozen in ice cubes. *I have one cube* in hot water every morning.

Decaf Twinings tea, water with lemon, the occasional glass of bubbles (Prosecco or champagne but not much).

99% of time I start with a glass of warm water, then I will have mint tea, or peppermint and ginger tea.

Watered down cranberry juice. Decaf flat white. Decaf tea with almond milk. *I like* fresh pineapple juice - reduces inflammation.

Decaff cappuccino with *So Good* High Protein Almond milk and a flavoured syrup (*Jordan's Skinny Syrup*).

Decaf coffee and tea. Any brand because it's hard to get. And my night-time drink is ginger and lemon tea. Sufficient water throughout the day.

Turmeric latte. Milk of choice, cinnamon stick, ½ teaspoon turmeric and a touch of black pepper and a sprinkle of cinnamon on top. Heat up in small saucepan, and especially great in the evening for rest.

My one and only (for the day) oat cappuccino.

A lovely glass of water.

That morning liquid...

Decaf oat flat white, turmeric almond latte, and *I still consume* caffeine in the form of soy matcha with honey. I start every day with a cup or two of fresh slices of lemon and fresh ginger in boiling water - it's wonderful - I know there are lemon and ginger teabags but I dislike teabags of any kind. Fresh is best.

I am obsessed with my soda stream. I usually add a dash of cranberry juice. It's quite a mild refreshing flavour.

Steeped fresh grated ginger and cinnamon in water every morning. Otherwise its just fresh squeezed lemon in water. *Sometimes I enjoy* a turmeric latte at the coffee shop with almond milk.

Ginger tea is great, I agree! *I also like* rosehip + hibiscus. But more than anything I drink *Rooibos* tea because it can be served with milk which is somehow the way I like my 'tea'. Also homemade kombucha!

Sometimes I enjoy a turmeric latte at the coffee shop with almond milk.

Organic apple cider vinegar with honey lemon ginger cardamom tea.

Instead of coffee, a lot of fresh ginger, add juice, frozen pineapple, frozen berries, soaked chia seeds, tea leaves from two green tea bags, parsley if you want to add, then blend... you can also add ¼ lemon with rind if you like. The ginger is good for inflammation and nausea.

Green tea because it *reduces inflammation* is overall great for the body.

Drinks throughout the Day

Just water. From the tap. From the fridge. With tinkling ice cubes in summer. Crushed ice is especially good when you're melting in the summer heat.

I steep fresh ginger in a coffee maker to make a jar of ginger water. I then mix some of that ginger water and some fresh lemon juice in with my one litre water bottle. It makes it a bit easier to drink all my water each day and provides an immune boost in winter. It helps with nausea, yes! Especially if you used it without the lemon juice and just used the ginger. As a recipe, it would look something like 'roughly chop a 3-4 cm piece of ginger, pour in approximately two cups of boiling water into a coffee plunger, steep for 24 hours. After the water has cooled, transfer to fridge. If you don't have a coffee plunger, any tea strainer and container sufficient to hold two cups will work. For a stronger infusion, reduce the amount of water. After 24 hours, pour liquid into a clean, sealable jar. Use liquid in hot or cold water either on its own or in combination with fresh lemon juice, a cinnamon quill in the infusion, or a small amount of honey to treat colds, help boost immunity, treat nausea or to help increase fluid intake if you are struggling with plain water.'

I have steeped fresh grated ginger and cinnamon in water every morning. Otherwise its just fresh squeezed lemon in water.

Peppermint tea, soda with cranberry, soda with ginger syrup (sugar free).

In winter, I have cups of tea throughout the day, and water.

I'm suuuuper boring and in winter, I drink hot water instead of cold water to keep my water intake up. Sometimes I get tired of flavours in the water and really tired of cold water but hot water works well. Sometimes with lemon too and herbs like mint.

I have a Milo or hot chocolate for morning tea. Otherwise a juice and water, flavoured water helps me drink more.

Water. Coke (no sugar). Iced tea. Soda water.

When it's hot, I like a soft drink (they generally contain low amounts of sodium) with ice.

Lemon Iced Tea (7mg sodium).

I love to have a fresh fruit smoothie sometime during the day. I throw in some strawberries, blueberries, watermelon, and banana, 1 cup of ice cold milk (or plain yoghurt) and honey to taste into a blender and process until smooth. Pour it into a glass and slurp!

My Drinks

_____
_____
_____
_____
_____
_____
_____
_____
_____
_____
_____
_____

Lunch

Lunch. *Traditionally* a meal eaten in the middle of the day, and usually a light meal.

But listen to your body.

If you want your lunch as the main meal, and dinner as the lighter meal, *then go for it*. Again, to be kind to yourself to lessen your Ménière's symptoms, opt for *fresh foods*, not packaged. *Limit salt* and *sugar intake* as it can cause water retention, which affects your inner ear and worsens your Ménière's symptoms.

Savoring the good thymes at lunch.

Today's forecast: 100% chance of deliciousness at lunch.

It is more fun to talk with someone who doesn't use long, difficult words but rather short, easy words like "What about lunch?" - A.A. Milne

Lunch

I make traditional soup consisting of a flavorful broth, rice noodles, herbs, and various meats like beef or chicken, using the spices pack from Low Sodium Foods Australia.

A bowl of mixed salad either homemade or one of the supermarket packs.

Mini pizza base with avocado and melted cheese (*Norco Natural* usually), or cottage or ricotta cheese.

When at home, I don't have a designated lunch moment as *I tend to graze* throughout the day on fruit, homemade muffins or even have a breakfast cereal for lunch.

Unsalted pan-fried chicken breast or steamed chicken drumsticks, or unsalted mince meat with veggies (celery, carrots, peas and sweet corn). Woolies sell the frozen mix. Or unsalted pork rashers, unsalted baked salmon, unsalted egg on toast with avocado - all go with unsalted baked potatoes (high in potassium), steam veggies and sometimes with baked pumpkin. *I get creative and add* curry powder, smoked paprika, garlic, onion powder, cumin, oregano, thyme, tons of pepper, etc put any cut chicken and mashed potato on low-sodium wraps to go. Use smashed avocado with tons of pepper as base and *I add* honey sometimes.

Low-salt tinned salmon, homemade mayo and chopped up low salt gherkins, pepper of course. Put on sourdough or fresh bread.

Corn Thins, Cruskits with poached chicken breast avocado tomato or tuna etc. Mushrooms on a piece of toast. Or the no name french fries at Woolies and Coles are *very low in salt* if you're Ménière's is active.

Salad. Or roast chicken and low-salt mayo.

Yoghurt, boiled egg, rice. Fruit.

Avocado on toast with olive oil and black pepper. *I make my own* bread which makes it even better low-salt wise.

Homemade schnitzel, steak or fish on rice with some veggies or salad.

All my meals are all based around a low salt intake. Also caffeine limited to decaf half-strength cappuccino. *Water intake should be very good.* Eat no processed foods as they are full of sugar and salt.

Wraps made with my own homemade wraps. Salads.

Home made soups. Something fast - eggs.

Peanut butter and celery. Low-salt cheese and avocado.

Eat real food farm not factory and you will be fine!

I like homemade flat bread wrap with avocado, a protein (chicken, left over lamb or beef or baby bocconcini, lettuce & other salad stuff).

Homemade minestrone soup, usually left over from a dinner, or pumpkin etc.

I try not to eat bread unless I make my own. Potato cooked in microwave filled with coleslaw or tomato and leftover mince.

No-added salt canned tuna in spring water, drained and mixed with sour cream and dill.

Lunch

Wraps, chicken, avocado, tomato, cucumber, spinach leaves and little dressing of your choice. One slice sourdough bread with avocado or egg. Add your favourite topping.

I make a batch of soup each week in winter, which I have with either quinoa or brown rice. Add cannellini beans or lentils for extra protein. I use *Maggie Beer* stock, which yields a manageable salt portion per serving (you still need some salt).

Salad and poached chicken is my go to... homemade dressing too with no added salt.

Protein and salad or roast veggies with no salt.

Avocado and low-salt cottage cheese.

I like wholemeal pasta, spring onion, red and green capsicum, snow peas, *Maleny Cuisine* Sweet Chilli Sauce - cook pasta as per instructions, cut up veggie and add to pasta and drizzle over sweet chilli sauce to your liking. I usually make enough for three days. Add what veggies you want.

My lunch usually consists of fruit and/or nuts, and a chai latte.
Caffeine is one of my primary triggers!

I love a pasta salad – penne pasta or shell pasta when I'm thinking of a sea change, or bow tie pasta to feel fancy. I add peas, zest and juice of a lemon, olive oil, some cooked chicken, cherry tomatoes, or pumpkin.

Just poached eggs, tomato, leftover veggies and low-salt flat bread.

Avocado is a star! Add tomato, chicken, lettuce all stacked on some low-salt bread and I'm in for a treat. Sometimes I add low-salt mayo.

Simply a salad sandwich. Lettuce, grated carrot, sliced cucumber, capsicum, smashed avocado. *I add* low-sodium hummus if I feel brave.

A rainbow bowl. *I throw* a bounty of colourful salad items into a bowl, add a bit of *Red Kelly's* salad dressing and tuck in.

Fruit salad, *especially in summer*.

I wrap carrot sticks, avocado, low salt cheese, some chicken strips, cucumber and sliced beetroot in a leaf of lettuce.

I found poached chicken with rocket, raspberry vinaigrette and avocado on *taste.com.au*. It's wonderful in the hot weather.

Leftovers from the night before!

Bread is quite salty. *So often I'll have* a small tin of tuna, (or some tofu) beans, salad, maybe some buckwheat or rice crackers. Yoghurt and fruit later.

Zucchini Pancakes

makes: 7 fritters **prep:** 20 minutes **cooking time:** 5 minutes

When my husband is at home for lunch, we make this together. You know, like, I grab the ingredients from the fridge and the pantry and throw them at him, cause he loves when I challenge him like that (the intense look of concentration as to when the next ingredient is coming his way is so worth it!) He cooks. I eat. Perfect! - Julieann

Ingredients

- 2 cups grated zucchini
- 2 large eggs, slightly beaten
- 2 tablespoons chopped green onion
- ½ cup plain flour
- ¼ cup grated reduced salt cheese
- ½ teaspoon baking powder
- 1 pinch dried oregano
- ¼ cup vegetable oil, or as needed

low-sodium sour cream for serving (optional)

Method

1. Grate the zucchini, then use paper towel to remove moisture. Transfer into a large bowl.
2. Add eggs and green onion to the zucchini, and mix together.
3. In a separate bowl, stir cheese, flour, baking powder, and oregano together.
4. Add to zucchini mixture and stir, until batter is just moistened.
5. Add olive oil to a large fry pan set on medium heat. When the oil is hot, scoop 3 tablespoon fulls of the zucchini mixture into the pan, pressing them lightly into a round shape.
6. Cook the zucchini fritters for 2 to 3 minutes, then flip them once and cook an additional 2 minutes until golden brown and cooked throughout.
7. Place the zucchini fritters on to a paper towel-lined plate.
8. Repeat the cooking process with the remaining zucchini mixture.
9. Serve the zucchini fritters, topped with low-sodium sour cream (optional).

I love to add some Beerenberg Australian Fruit Chutney on the side. Delicious!

No-Salt Bread

makes: 10-12 **prep:** 10 minutes **cooking time:** 5 minutes

I was sick of turning over packets of wraps in supermarkets to check sodium levels, always hopeful, always disappointed. So I came up with my own no-salt bread after doing some Internet research. It works! ~ Sally

Ingredients

- 1 cup flour
- ½ cup Greek yoghurt
- 2 tablespoons olive oil or other oil. Bran oil is good.

That is all. The yoghurt gives it a flavour that commercial no-salt flatbreads/wraps don't have. No resemblance to cardboard!

Method

1. Mix the ingredients together, roll out on a lightly floured board.
2. Cook in a lightly oiled pan on both sides.

Freezes extremely well. I store it in the freezer in large ziplock bags with a piece of baking paper between each so it is easy to remove one at a time.

I love it served with roasted carrot chunks and steamed green beans.

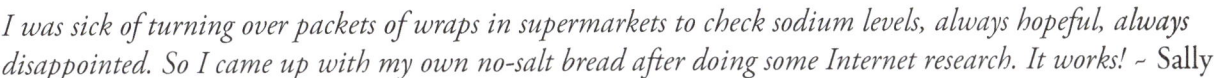

Homemade Bread

serves: 1 loaf **prep:** 1 hour 15 minutes **cooking time:** 30 minutes

When I was 9, I used to make homemade bread for my Barbie dolls. It was just flour and water back then, hoping the Barbie dolls would eat it and when I woke the next day, they would be alive! My bread is real now! When the kids were toddlers in my early Ménière's years, I had a breadmaker machine. Now I just use the oven - Julieann

Ingredients

- 2½ to 3 cups plain flour
- 1 package dry yeast
- 1 tablespoon sugar
- 1 cup warm water
- 1 tablespoon oil

Method

1. In a large mixing bowl, add the yeast, the sugar and just 1 cup of flour.
2. Pour in the oil and warm water, and mix for around 2 minutes.
3. Add the rest of the flour, bit by bit until the dough is no longer sticky.
4. On a floured surface, knead the bread for about 5 minutes. It should become smooth and stretchy.
5. Grease a bowl with a little oil, and put the dough into it.
6. Cover with clingwrap for around 30 minutes, or maybe less, depending on how hot the day is until it is doubled in size.
7. Gently push the dough down, shape into a loaf and pop it into a bread loaf tin. Cover with a clean tea towel and leave it for another 30 minutes or maybe less, depending on how hot the day is until it is doubled in size..
8. Remove the tea towel and transfer it to an oven (200º C) for around 30 minutes.
9. The bread is baked when it is a golden-brown colour (if the crust is pale, the inside may be raw). Tapping the bottom of the loaf should sound hollow.

Lemon Pepper Chicken with Risoni Salad

serves: 4 **prep:** 15 minutes **cooking time:** 7-10 minutes

I have seen this one in the "healthy food guide" but this is my version of it, I've added more ingredients etc… and theirs had feta in it, which I omitted obviously ~ Kim

Ingredients

- chicken tenderloins
- no-added salt lemon pepper seasoning
- 2 lemons, halved
- ½ cup Risoni
- 120g baby rocket, rinsed
- 1 punnet of cherry tomatoes, halved
- 2 small cucumbers, halved length-ways and diced
- baby corn, halved length-ways, or no-added salt corn kernels
- olive oil

Method

1. Cook Risoni as per directions, drain and refresh under cold water. Drain and transfer to a large bowl.
2. Coat the chicken in the seasoning, heat olive oil in a non-stick pan and cook chicken over a medium heat, until cooked through.
3. In a small fry pan, over high heat, place lemons cut side down and cook for 3 minutes until golden and slightly softened.
4. Add rocket, corn, tomatoes, cucumber to the bowl containing the Risoni.
5. Drizzle with 1 tablespoon of olive oil and toss to combine.

Serve with the chicken sliced & lemon halves.

Nick's Butter Chicken

serves: 4 **prep:** 15 minutes **cooking time:** 20 minutes

Even when I attend family meals, BBQs etc I always have to bring something I can eat and hubby's nephew decided one night he would make this for me from scratch, he loves cooking, and I felt included, and it really made me feel amazing and it was delicious. He's a sweetheart, he always thinks of Aunty Kimmy and where possible includes me in the menu. Love ya, Nick x

Ingredients

- 500g diced chicken
- 25g unsalted butter, approx.
- 1 onion
- crushed garlic, to taste
- 1 teaspoon each of: pepper, turmeric, Garam Masala.
- ½ teaspoon each of: chilli flakes, chilli powder, cinnamon, cloves, paprika
- ¼ teaspoon each of: oregano and sage
- 1 sachet of no-added salt tomato paste
- thickened cream to taste

Method

1. Pan fry diced chicken in butter, adding extra butter as chicken is cooking, if required.
2. Mix spices all together and add along with tomato paste.
3. Simmer until cooked and slightly thickened. Add cream when serving.
4. Serve with rice.

Great heated up for lunch the next day!

Pasta Salad

serves: 4 **prep:** 15 minutes **cooking time:** 15 minutes

Uncle Charlie inspired this recipe. He always made the dressing for when we had a BBQ or lunch at his place with my grandparents. It has lots of fond memories attached where we listened to many stories of their travels. He was an avid photographer and loved wildflowers, so this dressing always reminds me of those happy times ~ Kim.

Ingredients

Pasta Salad 1

- 1½ cups cooked pasta
- ¼ cup spring onions, chopped
- 2 tablespoons parsley, chopped
- 2 sticks celery, diced
- 2 tablespoons no-added salt corn kernels
- 2 red or green capsicums, diced
- sultanas, if desired
- cherry tomatoes (optional)
- add protein if you like (chicken, tuna, eggs, turkey, salmon, chickpeas)

Pasta Salad 2

Combine cooked pasta of choice with:
- cherry tomatoes cut in half
- snow peas
- can of no-added salt corn kernels or lightly cooked frozen corn kernels
- sliced mushrooms (if desired)
- dress with your favourite low-sodium dressing.

Method

1. Combine all dressing ingredients in an airtight container.
2. Shake well and pour over salad ingredients.

Dressing:
- ½ cup olive oil
- 1 tablespoon sugar
- ¼ cup vinegar
- 1-2 teaspoons curry powder

Singapore Noodles

serves: 2 **prep:** 10 minutes **cooking time:** 15 minutes

Hubby loves Singapore Noodles from the local Chinese place & of course I'm jealous as I can't eat them, so I created this recipe so I could feel like I was having takeaway too. Buy some noodle boxes and pretend properly! It's also delicious reheated the next day for a leftovers lunch.

Ingredients

- 1 pack of Singapore noodles, low sodium
- 2 spring onions, chopped
- ½ red capsicum, diced
- 10 snow peas, thinly sliced
- 1 tablespoon olive oil
- handful of bean sprouts, washed
- ½ teaspoon of low-sodium curry powder
- 1 tablespoon of low-sodium Worcestershire sauce

Method

1. Boil kettle, put noodles into bowl and pour over with boiling water. Leave for 5 minutes, strain.
2. Heat oil in wok.
3. Add capsicum and stir fry for 3 minutes.
4. Add spring onions and snow peas and stir fry for 1 minute.
5. Add bean sprouts, curry powder and drained noodles.
6. Stir well to combine and cook for a further 2 minutes.
7. Add Worcestershire sauce and serve.

Simple, long life Salad Dressing

serves: many **prep:** 5 minutes **cooking time:** 0 minutes

Kim kindly sent in this no-salt, long life salad dressing that lasts for ages in the pantry. It complements any salad with a touch of freshness and sweetness. The salt-free French Onion Soup is quite versatile and can be used as a flavour enhancer, or just as a soup.

Ingredients

- 1 cup olive oil
- 1 cup honey
- 1 cup vinegar
- 1 teaspoon curry powder (or to taste)
- 1 teaspoon crushed garlic (or to taste)
- ¼ teaspoon crushed black pepper

Method

1. Add the ingredients into airtight container and shake to combine.

Lasts for ages in the pantry, *don't refrigerate.*

Salt Free French Onion Soup Mix

Ingredients

- 2⅔ tablespoons dried onion flakes
- 4 teaspoons *Salt Skip* beef stock powder
- 1 teaspoon onion powder
- ¼ teaspoon celery seed
- ½ teaspoon garlic powder

Method

1. Combine all ingredients.

Great for adding to a potato bake, or just handy to have made up in a airtight container to add flavour to casseroles etc, or a simple soup to enjoy for lunch.

- Add ¼ cup dry soup mix to 2 cups of water to make a soup.

My Favourite Salad Lunch

makes: 1 **prep:** 10 minutes **cooking time:** 0 minutes

This is ridgy-didge my favourite salad lunch because it contains all my favourite ingredients, and I love jamming in everything! It's crunchy, healthy, and refreshing ~ Sally

Ingredients

- half of 1 mixed prepared salad bowl
- salad and vegetable ingredients from the fridge - whatever you like
- a handful of unsalted nuts e.g. cashews, walnuts, peanuts
- dressing of choice
- side of hummus

Easy No-Salt Hummus

- 1 x 425mg can of chick peas - *no added* salt
- 1 good sized clove of garlic
- ¾ cup of tahini paste (hulled). *Tahini is sesame seed based.*
- 1 tablespoon of lemon juice
- a dash of olive oil - about a teaspoon
- 2 pinches of paprika
- flat-leaf parsley to garnish

1. Put everything into a food processor or blender and puree until smooth.
2. Taste. If there is anything you'd prefer more of - garlic, lemon juice, paprika - don't be afraid to add it!

Method

1. I start with a pre-packed supermarket mixed, but undressed salad. I use half, so one mix lasts for two meals, or it's a lunch for two. My current favourite is the *Green Goodness Salad Kit* from Woolies. It includes dried cranberries and sunflower seeds, edamame beans as well as wombok, broccoli, cabbage, corn and kale. But you can start with any salad, or if you're not in a hurry, make your own base.
2. Then add items from the fridge, which can vary depending what there is. Today I used tomato, red capsicum, avocado, cucumber and a few grapes. Often I'll add a few unsalted walnuts, cashews or peanuts as well.
3. Because I like some protein with the salad, using up left over cooked chicken, or hard boiled egg is common. This day I used *Woolies Cherry Bocconcini*, a soft cheese very low in sodium.
4. Dress the salad with whatever you like - oil and vinegar, or perhaps a low-sodium dressing like those made by *Red Kelly's* (available in supermarkets or at lowsodiumfoods.com.au).

Add some home made no-salt hummus on the side.

Sandwiches

makes: 1 **prep**: varies **cooking time**: depends on ingredients

Bread - your choice of wholegrain, wholemeal, sourdough - checking for sodium content to be less than 400mg per 100g.

Hummus & Veggie Sanga

¼ cup sliced cucumber, 3 tablespoons hummus, ¼ medium red bell pepper, sliced, ¼ avocado, mashed, ½ cup mixed salad greens, ¼ cup shredded carrot.

Tzatziki, Superfood Slaw & Grilled Fish Sanga

Tzatziki - finely grated cucumber, Greek yoghurt, black pepper, ½ teaspoon lemon zest - mix. Cod fillets - fried or baked to your liking - add garlic or ginger or turmeric if you like. Superfood Slaw from the supermarket or make your own, add 2 tablespoons lemon juice and 1 teaspoon of honey.

Pineapple & Grilled Chicken

Homemade sodium-free bread with almond spread, or avocado as a base, then add salad, four bean mix (packet low sodium), and pineapple, grilled chicken.

Choose Your Filling...

Low-salt canned tuna or salmon. Low-salt cheese. Eggs. Grilled chicken with grilled red capsicums (remove the skin). Avocado or salad sandwiches.

Low-Sodium Sandwich Stack

Slice of bread (no crust if you like), spread of reduced-salt cottage cheese, no-added salt salmon. Slice of bread, spread of reduced-salt cottage cheese, slices of cucumber. Slice of bread, mashed avocado. Finish with a slice of bread.

Refreshing Apple and Cheese

Thinly sliced apple (of your choice) with layers of Swiss cheese on top. Tasty and refreshing!

Change it up Salad

serves: 3-4 **prep:** 10 minutes **cooking time:** 0 minutes

Green salads can be well... salad. But your salad can be... SALAD with a zoomba! Here's some ideas to change up your salad. There's loads of tasty salad recipes online as well, just check the sodium content.

Delight in your dressing

Change up your salad by using a variety of low-sodium salad dressings:
- Sweet Mustard Salad Dressing
- Italian Style Salad Dressing
- Attitude Salad Dressing
- Thai Style Salad Dressing
- Basil and Garlic Dressing
- Lemon Myrtle Dressing
- Sweet Chilli & Lime Dressing
- Smooth Tangy Traditional Dressing

(*lowsodiumfoods.com.au*) Or make your own salad dressing from recipes online

Vary Flavours and Textures

Veggies
Add roasted potato, roasted sweet potato, roasted pumpkin, kidney beans, green beans, peas, raw broccoli, corn kernels, cucumber, cabbage, brussel sprouts, cauliflower, snow peas, radishes, carrot, capsicum, zucchini

Fruit
Grapefruit, pear, grated apple, thin apple slices, orange segments, mango, cranberries, tomatoes, nectarines, watermelon, grapes, peach, lychee, starfruit, strawberries

Nuts
Sunflower seeds, pistachios, pepitas, walnuts, pecans, cashew, hazelnuts, almonds

Greens
Rocket, kale, iceberg lettuce, cos lettuce, baby spinach leaves, butter lettuce, watercress

Other additions
Honey, apple cider vinegar, herbs like tarragon, rosemary, thyme, pasta, grains like quinoa, couscous, rice, pearl barley, low-sodium dijon mustard, honey mustard, mayonnaise, Greek yoghurt, balsamic, sweet plum dressing

Add Healthy Fats

For a more satisfying salad, add low-sodium cheeses, avocado, beans, chicken, lamb, beef, turkey, low-sodium tuna, salmon, egg

Hemp Seed Tabbouleh

serves: 4 **prep:** 10 minutes **cooking time:** 0 minutes

Andy gave us this fabulous Tabbouleh recipe that she makes. Historically, it's a traditional Lebanese or Syrian side dish or salad and is made with Bulgar wheat. Andy's recipe doesn't contain Bulgar wheat, so it's perfect as a gluten-free dish.

Ingredients

- 1 cup of parsley, very finely chopped without stalks
- 2 tablespoons fresh mint, finely chopped
- 2 tablespoons olive oil
- juice of half a lemon
- 2 roma tomatoes or half a punnet baby romas - sweet and less juice
- 1 cup of hemp seeds
- a little white pepper
- lite salt which is potassium chloride, not sodium chloride. This doesn't trigger me.

Method

1. Mix the olive oil, lemon juice, salt (optional) together.
2. Throw in the parsley, tomatoes, hemp seeds, mint and a little white pepper and mix.
3. Taste. Balance flavours to your liking.

I don't add red onion, as I am intolerant of onion & garlic. Some people do, but it is actually not traditional.

Zucchini, Mushroom and Ricotta Pasta Sauce

serves: 4 **prep:** 15 minutes **cooking time:** 20 minutes

Francoise submitted this lovely dish to us. It has its origins with Italian home recipes, sometimes also known as the ultimate restaurant-quality vegetarian dish.

Ingredients

- 1 spanish onion chopped in half slices
- 1 garlic finely chopped
- 2 small to medium zucchini sliced
- 6 mushrooms sliced
- 1 x 250g no-added salt ricotta cheese
- 1 tablespoon mixed herbs
- ¼ cup dry medium sherry
- ¼ cup water
- 1 teaspoon cornflour & ¼ cup cold water
- juice from 1 lemon

Method

1. Sauté onion and garlic until onions are soft, stir often.
2. Add sherry and stir for a minutes
3. Add water, zucchini and mushrooms and stir. Let it steam and stir occasionally. When zucchini are almost soft, turn off heat if electric stove or turn down low for gas.
4. Mix cornflour and cold water. Add to zucchini and mushroom mixture and stir for a couple of minutes.
5. Add in the ricotta cheese and mix in well.
6. Then add the lemon juice and pepper and stir.
Serve with pasta and a green salad.

Pasta & Pesto

serves: 4 **prep:** 15 minutes **cooking time:** pasta 12 minutes

Ingredients

- 1 bunch fresh basil leaves (removed from stem) (about 2 cups packed)
- 2 cloves garlic
- ½ cup pine nuts, walnuts, almonds or combination
- ½ cup grated no added salt cheese, or try 300g no-added salt ricotta cheese
- ½ cup olive oil
- juice of half lemon and pepper

Method

1. Combine all ingredients in a blender.
2. Blend until a smooth paste.
Toss through hot pasta. Enjoy!

Tuna/Salmon Garden Salad

serves: 1 **prep:** 10 minutes **cooking time:** 0 minutes

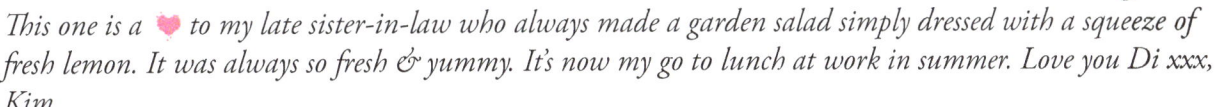

This one is a 💗 to my late sister-in-law who always made a garden salad simply dressed with a squeeze of fresh lemon. It was always so fresh & yummy. It's now my go to lunch at work in summer. Love you Di xxx, Kim

Ingredients

Coz lettuce leaves topped with:
- cherry tomatoes
- slices of cucumber
- sliced capsicum
- sliced snow peas
- sliced mushrooms (if desired)
- low-sodium tuna or salmon
- low-sodium sun-dried tomatoes

Method

1. Mix all ingredients

Drizzle with favourite salad dressing or just lemon juice and enjoy.

* Easy to prepare in the morning before work, take dressing in leak proof jar in your lunchbox.

Rice Cake Toppings

- no-added salt peanut butter topped with sliced banana and a drizzle of honey
- low-sodium tuna or salmon mixed with homemade mayo and no-added salt corn, sprinkle with chives
- mashed avocado, topped with fresh tomato and loads of cracked black pepper
- hardboiled egg (mashed and mix with homemade mayo and chives)
- spread homemade mayo over rice cake and top with fresh tomato, cracked black pepper and slices of avocado if in season.

Jacket Potatoes ~ 3 Ways

serves: 1 **prep:** 15 minutes **cooking time:** 20 minutes

Jacket potatoes can be traced back to South America, where potatoes originated. Jacket spuds were used in coat pockets as hand warmers by those going to work or school in the 18th and 19th centuries in the UK. It became a street food in 19th century Britain. Thanks to Francois for these three versions of jacket potatoes.

Version 1

Ingredients

- 1 whole medium potato, cooked in 220° C oven (50 minutes) or microwave (8-12 minutes) until tender.
- 1 teaspoon chopped parsley
- 30g shredded *Salt Skip* shredded cheese
- white pepper
- ¼ cup corn kernels

Method

1. When potato is cooked, carefully scoop out potato inside leaving 'shell' intact.
2. Mash and add ingredients, combine.
3. Spoon mixture back into shell and top with cheese and cook in oven for 15-20 minutes.

Version 2

Top cooked jacket potato with homemade coleslaw and *Salt Skip* shredded cheese.

Version 3

Top cooked jacket potato with low-sodium baked beans and *Salt Skip* shredded cheese.

Corn Chowder

serves: 4 **prep:** 15 minutes **cooking time:** 30 minutes

My dad's brother, Uncle Doug, would visit about 3 or 4 times during the year. Each time, he would cook a creamed corn for us all at breakfast. I always enjoyed it with toast. When this recipe for Corn Chowder came in from Francoise, it reminded me of Uncle Doug. Corn chowder is said to have originated with French and English seafarers in North America and then it appeared in recipes in the US around 1884.

Ingredients

- 1 tablespoon unsalted butter or oil
- 2 brown onions, chopped
- ¼ cup plain flour
- 3 cups milk
- 2 cups no-added salt chicken stock
- 1kg frozen corn kernels
- 500g unpeeled potatoes, cut into 2cm cubes
- 2 teaspoons dried thyme

Method

1. Melt butter in pan over medium heat and add onion, cook 3-4 minutes or until onion is tender.
2. Add flour, stirring constantly, cook for 1 minute.
3. Combine milk and stock and add to pan stirring constantly to ensure there are no lumps.
4. Bring to boil, add corn, potatoes, thyme, pepper.
5. Simmer for 15-20 minutes or until potatoes are cooked through.

Great for lunches as it freezes well.

Summertime Lunch

serves: 1 **prep:** 10 minutes **cooking time:** 0 minutes

- 1 cup yogurt
- fresh berries, whatever is in season (can use frozen)
- ½ cup muesli or clusters

Top yogurt with cluster/muesli, add berries and enjoy.

My Lunches

Feeling Snackish

Everyone likes to grab a *quick snack* at some time during the day.
Except, when you have Ménière's, grabbing a commercialised,
pre-packaged snack can set off a trail of unwanted Ménière's symptoms,
due to high salt, added salt, hidden salts, high sugar,
sugar substitutes & other additives. Artificial sweeteners like aspartame,
are listed as a common dietary trigger for Ménière's. They can cause, trigger
or worsen symptoms as they increase the concentration of substances
in the inner ear, affecting the fluid balance.

Be kind to yourself:
- Eat snacks at a *regular time*.
- Aim for *homemade*, and *fresh fruit, vegetables* and *whole grains*.
- Stay *well-hydrated*, to flush salts and toxins from your system.

Popcorn is one of the only situations
in which you eat the result of an explosion.

The peculiar habit, when searching for a snack,
of constantly returning to the refrigerator
in hopes that something new will have materialized.

Because the bond of friendship
gets even stronger over snacks.

Feeling Snackish

Mmmm... home-popped popcorn!

Any fruit that is in season. Fresh dates.

I like unsalted Premium crackers with tomato and low-salt cheese.

Unsalted potato chips. Unsalted nuts and seeds.

Gluten-free bread as Fairy Bread ~ *always a big kid*.

Fruit salad with a dollop of dairy-free yoghurt.

Unsalted cashews. Dark chocolate - 85% cocoa.

I love to eat Sao crackers with butter and cheese, an apple, handful of almonds, banana, small tin of tuna.

Watermelon, cantaloupe, honeydew and cucumber slices.

Activia yoghurt. It's sweetened with stevia (a 'safe' sweetener). *I freeze the little 125g ones and eat them frozen like little ice blocks.* There are several flavours to choose from.

Muesli bars.

Arnott's Snack Right Oaty Bites (Cocoa and Oat) - 76mg sodium/100g.

Frozen berries, ice, water and protein powder - low-sodium.

Nuts, dates with peanut butter, protein smoothie or protein ball.

Microwave poppadoms are the best. Or corn thins with cheese. Or nuts.

Lately my dopamine is raspberries with vanilla coconut yoghurt (and to *appease my inner child*, I buy the pouch ones and squeeze a little yoghurt in each raspberry one at a time lol). Makes it take longer too!

Dried apricots as very low in salt, and nibble on Sunrice Thin Rice Cakes - also very low in salt.

The Mayver's 'smunchy' unsalted peanut butter. *I roast* almonds and they are great to nibble on!

Greek yoghurt with strawberries or a dribble of raw honey.

Raw veggies with dip - carrots, celery, capsicum, cucumber, broccoli.

Summer fruit skewers.

I nibble on ginger cubes when I'm feeling nauseous.

No-salt crackers with slices of apple.

Feeling Snackish

Low-sodium rice cakes with hardboiled egg.

Sliced apples dipped in low-sodium peanut butter. ☺

Loaded rice cakes - low-fat cottage cheese and tomato on top. Or avocado. Or cucumber. Or capsicum.

Frozen fruit smoothie.

I squeeze blood oranges and freeze them in the little silicon Popsicle molds.

Guacamole and salt-free corn chips.

Marshmallows. That's all.

Best snack I know: Place a whole almond in the centre of a single piece of dried apricot. Eat. *Yummm!*

Celery sticks with peanut butter.

Homemade muffins.

Toast with banana and cinnamon.

Fruit, dried apricots, no added sodium rice crackers, sesame snaps, muesli bars, nuts.

Roasted unsalted nuts.

A bunch of grapes; or cherries etc depending on season.

Unsalted nuts of all kinds.

Chunks of Norco Natural cheese.

The top handful of chips from the lowest sodium chips going - partner eats the rest. The salt settles to the bottom in the bag, lol!

The crackers on *Low-sodium Foods* with unsalted butter and slices of tomato with pepper.

Homemade trail mix.

Granola bars.

Mango. Nothing better!

Baked salt-reduced wraps with cinnamon and sugar.

Chocolate Coconut Go To Snacks

serves: 12 **prep:** 10 minutes **cooking time:** 0 minutes

Merilyn sent in this recipe for 'feeling snackish'. She said, 'These are just delicious. It's hard not to stop at four of them!' I had to make them being a chocoholic, so I go to it. And Merilyn was right. It is hard to stop at four of them. So I ate eight. Of course I didn't regret it!

Ingredients

- 2 cups dates
- ½ cup coconut
- ¼ cup cacao
- 1½ cups almond meal
- peanut butter or coconut oil

This recipe is basic. Add different ingredients if you like.

Method

1. Put all ingredients in food processor until smooth and well combined.
2. Roll into balls and coat with coconut.
3. Put into fridge, they keep for ages and are a great choice for a sweet snack.

The Carrot Bread of Hidden Apple

serves: 10 **prep:** 15 minutes **cooking time:** 45 minutes

*I bake this when I want to keep a snack longer than an hour. My kids generally don't eat it because (a) it's **too** healthy, or (b) they suddenly don't like carrot in cake, or (c) apple is a fruit and you don't cook fruit, or (d) they're too full (from what, I don't know!). I don't tell them it's delicious! ~Julieann ~ P.S. My daughter who HATES cooked apple had a slice. She commented how nice it was, as I chuckled to myself about the cooked apple in it. I'm hoping she doesn't read this cookbook. Eeeek!*

Ingredients

- 1 cup self-raising flour
- ¾ cup peeled, grated carrots
- ¾ cup peeled, grated red apples
- ¼ cup sour cream, or light sour cream, or Greek yoghurt
- ⅓ cup coconut oil, canola or vegetable oil
- ½ cup packed light brown sugar
- 1 large egg
- ¼ cup white sugar
- ½ teaspoon ground nutmeg
- 2 teaspoons vanilla extract
- 2 teaspoons cinnamon

Add chocolate chips or nuts or seeds if you like.

Method

1. Preheat oven to 180º C.
2. Grease a loaf pan with olive oil cooking spray, or rub butter in the pan with a light dusting of flour. In a large bowl, add sour cream, coconut oil, light brown sugar, egg, white sugar, nutmeg, vanilla extract, cinnamon.
3. Add the flour, and fold with spatula or wooden spoon until just combined.
4. Fold in the carrots and apples.
5. Turn thick batter into the pan, smoothing the top lightly.
6. Bake for around 45 minutes, or until the top is golden and the center is set
7. Allow the bread to cool in pan for about 15 minutes before turning it out onto a cool rack.
8. Slice and enjoy as is, or with butter on top.

Date and Pumpkin Loaf

serves: 10-12 **prep:** 20 minutes **cooking time:** 40-45 minutes

This recipe is one I made up and seems to have gone down well with those that have tasted it. It came about when I had some pumpkin hanging about and it was either use it now or throw it away. There was not enough for a pumpkin loaf, so decided to add the dates to get the bulk ~ Francoise

Ingredients

- 150g chopped pumpkin
- 1 cup of chopped dates
- 1 cinnamon stick
- ½ cup of water
- ½ cup vegetable or light olive oil
- ¼ cup brown sugar
- ¼ cup golden syrup
- 2 eggs
- ¾ cup wholemeal flour
- 1¼ cup plain flour
- 1½ teaspoons sodium bicarbonate
- ½ cup chopped pecans or walnuts

Method

1. Place pumpkin, dates, cinnamon stick and water into a saucepan.
2. Bring to boil and simmer gently on very low for 15 minutes or until pumpkin is cooked.
3. Remove cinnamon stick and allow to cool.
4. Mash pumpkin and dates.
5. Place oil and brown sugar into a bowl and mix well.
6. Add in golden syrup and mix well.
7. Add eggs one at a time and mix well.
8. Add cooled mashed pumpkin and date mixture and mix well.
9. Add sifted flours and bi-carb.
10. Add nuts and fold in gently.
11. Place in a loaf tin and bake in a moderate oven (180º C) for 45-50 minutes or until inserted knife or skewer comes out clean.

Allow to cool in tin for five minutes before removing.

Note: This will also make 12 muffins. For muffins cook for 12-20 minutes or until inserted knife or skewer comes out clean.

Hummus

serves: 6 **prep:** 10 minutes **cooking time:** 45 minutes

This recipe is also from Francoise. Hummus has an ancient history in the Middle East, perhaps around the 13th century. The addition of tahini emerged in Egypt. Hummus is widely used as a dip for vegetables nowadays, and can also be used as a spread on sandwiches and crackers.

Ingredients

- 3 cups well-cooked chickpeas
- 2 tablespoons lemon juice
- ¼ cup tehini (tahini)
- ¾ teaspoon ground coriander
- 2 cloves garlic
- ½ teaspoon ground cumin
- 1 tablespoon olive oil
- finely chopped parsley

Method

1. In a food processor blend all ingredients.
2. Add additional lemon juice or water to make the mixture a little more liquid.

Serve with veggie sticks and no-salt crackers.

Grandad's Peanut Biscuits

serves: 24 **prep:** 10 minutes **cooking time:** 10 minutes

I've included this recipe in memory of my father-in-law, who had Ménière's disease from in his late 20s. At the grand old age of 94, he could still hear with hearing aids! He loved to bake these peanut cookies, and they were always a treat ~ Julieann

Ingredients

- 1 cup of sugar
- 125g of butter
- 1 egg
- 1½ cups self-raising flour
- 1 cup of raw peanuts

Method

1. Preheat the oven to 180º C.
2. Using an electric mixer, beat the sugar and butter until the butter is lighter in colour.
3. Add the egg and mix.
4. Mix in the flour, slowly, and then the peanuts.
5. Place tablespoons of the mixture onto a lined tray, push down with a fork, and bake for 7-10 minutes until browned.

My kids love to eat them with a glass of milk. I love to eat them anytime, and sometimes I throw in some chocolate chips into the mixture.

Mini Blueberry Muffins

serves: 24 **prep:** 10 minutes **cooking time:** 25 minutes

When I'm baking muffins, cakes or biscuits, my kids appear out of nowhere. And then the biscuits or cakes disappear. Except the mini blueberry muffins because (a) my daughter doesn't like cooked fruit, (b) my youngest son doesn't like blueberries, which leaves one son, a husband, and me to share ~ Julieann

Ingredients

For the Muffins

- 2½ cups plain flour
- 1 cup sugar
- 2 eggs
- ½ cup unsalted butter
- ½ cup milk
- 1 teaspoon vanilla
- 1½ cups blueberries (fresh or frozen)

The Crumble on Top

- ⅓ cup plain flour
- ½ cup white sugar
- ¼ cup butter, cubed
- 1½ teaspoons ground cinnamon

Method

Muffin Batter

1. Preheat the oven to 180º C.
2. Grease a muffin tin or line with muffin papers.
3. In a small bowl mix the wet ingredients: eggs, vegetable oil, milk, vanilla extract.
4. Add the flour and sugar and stir well.
5. Fold the blueberries into the batter, taking care not to break the blueberries.
6. Spoon the batter into the muffin tin. It should fill the muffin cups to the top.

The Crumble on Top

1. Add the sugar, flour, cinnamon, and unsalted butter into a bowl and mix with a fork.
2. Place about a tablespoon over each muffin before baking.

Bake for 20 to 25 minutes.
Muffins will be ready when you can insert a toothpick into the center and it comes out clean.

My Go to Snacks

Dinner

Dinner

Research supports *eating dinner* between 5pm and 7pm, or at least 3 hours before you go to bed. It helps with better blood sugar regulation, improves metabolism, helps digestion, energy levels and *long term* health outcomes.
It also reduces the risk of weight gain.
While this is all good and dandy, realistically it might be hard to stick to this timing with busy family schedules,
but if you can, try to eat earlier in the evening.

For people with *Ménière's disease*,
it is recommended to try to eat the same amount of food,
and drink the same amount of fluid, *at about the same time every day*.
This helps reduce changes in the *fluid balance* in the inner ear.
And a *balanced meal* is recommended - vegetables, protein (meats), grains (rice, pasta, quinoa), healthy fats (olive oil, avocado etc).

I'm sorry for what I said
when I was hungry.
Give me food, and I'll be fine.

My kitchen's so clean,
it's almost science fiction.
Almost.

Kitchen decor tip:
Hide all evidence of last night's cooking disaster.

Dinner

White fish cooked with Nuttelex Butter - garlic and veggie salt blend, with air fryer potatoes and greens .

Cooked salmon lettuce tomatoes cucumber cross cheese two slices Kewpie mayo.

Chicken wings with cumin, paprika, garlic and onion powders, with Kewpie mayo (it's lower in sodium).

Steak broccolini asparagus tomato.

I love making my own food cause I can control the sodium levels and still enjoy great foods. But in saying so I love making soups, I get the no sodium or low-sodium broths cause I am personally too lazy to make my own broth but of course if you have the time then it's best to make your own. Other than that roast vegetables and meats I usually substitute the salt with paprika, garlic powder and pepper typically. And I love my seafood so garlic butter prawns, mushrooms with salmon or what ever fish you prefer, mash potatoes and green vegetables.

I take most recipes and just leave out the salt (if it uses it). I have celery powder, which has a great salty flavour. I also use *Herbie's Zalt*. I grow my own herbs, so I love using fresh herbs, and I dry my own herbs. Powdered garlic and onion add great flavouring and many other herbs and spices do too. Where you absolutely need salt (e.g. breads and doughs), I use good quality sea salt, in as minimum amount as required.

I like to eat a quinoa salad bowl - butter beans, cherry tomatoes, avocado, arugula (rocket), basil, and quinoa.

I've got MD and type 2 diabetes and my favourite dinner is 250mg of low carb chats from Woollies (25mg salt) a couple of large mushrooms peeled and the stems removed with 35g of Norco cheese on them which I cook in the oven at 180º C for 20 minutes with a piece of chicken thigh fillet cooked in the air fryer. If you have anyone in your family who doesn't have MD and likes mushrooms you can cook some for them on a separate tray and put some diced bacon on the mushrooms under the cheese. I also eat a salmon fillet with 150g of McCain healthy choice frozen chips, tomato and cucumber. Last night's dinner was a chicken thigh fillet with 300g of low carb chats which I boiled for 20 minutes, then browned them in a small frypan, and two fried eggs and cucumber and tomato as well.

Homemade pizza. *I just choose* a low-salt wrap or Lebanese bread for the base, roast some veggies, use low salt pesto or tomato paste.

Homemade veggie curry and Dahl, with homemade parathas and naan!

Sometimes I just have an avocado and a sprout sandwich (homemade bread).

I like to steam some vegetables and add them to plain pasta.

Dinner

Just cooked this. It's a mushroom and spinach crustless quiche. I used plant cream and my skip salt cheese and a little bit of mozzarella shredded (low sodium). I have fresh herbs in it too. Will go nice with a side of salad.

Spaghetti bolognese. *I make my own sauce* using no salt, and no-salt tomatoes. Plenty of garlic and herbs.

Homemade butter chicken. Just no salt added.

I make my own tortillas which I use to make chicken enchiladas.

Home made butter chicken and poached chicken.

I cook a lot of Mediterranean dishes and you can use garlic, onions, tomatoes and herbs and spices without adding salt. I do use some organic vegetable and or chicken stock powder from *San Elk* both only have 192mg sodium to 100mL of product but not the beef that has much more sodium. I use the powder in soups or mix it with oil and add it to my casseroles or I use it to marinate chicken etc with it.

Protein and salad and make my own dressing. Sometimes steamed veggies with a squeeze of lemon over the top. *Fresh is the way to go!*

For something simple, beef cubes and vegetable kebabs with salad on the side.

I make homemade hamburgers: 500g mince, 1 onion diced, 2 tablespoons *Spice Road Spices* Meatball & Mince seasoning, 1 egg, 1 teaspoon crushed garlic. Combine into patties and rest in fridge before BBQing.

Chicken and lentil casserole made with low-sodium chicken broth.

In summer, I love fish with lemon slices, wrapped in foil, baked in the oven.

I love a homemade pizza. *I make my own* pizza dough, then add my toppings of chicken, red onion, mushrooms, tomato, capsicum, no added salt tomato paste, basil, mozzarella cheese.

Toasties when I've had a big day. *I bake my own* low-salt bread and love avocado, chicken and quark cheese with the smallest dab of mayo.

Steak sandwiches. Homemade toasted bread, thinly sliced steak - pan-fried, cos lettuce, tomato, avocado. That's it. Sometimes I add BBQ sauce. Just a drop.

I like to experiment a little. I cooked chicken strips in some lime juice with some pepper, then added the cooked chicken to a bowl of baby spinach, snap peas, red onion, some pecans, fresh strawberries sliced in half, and my own dressing.

Lamb ragu with low-salt pasta. *I use* no-added salt tomato paste, use tomatoes from my veggie patch, and add onion, celery, carrot, and red grape juice instead of red wine.

Sometimes I just have a loaded plate of roasted veggies! So good!

Chicken kebabs with satay sauce and garden salad. Yum!

Most non-crustacean fish is low-sodium and *I cook* ocean trout or salmon with ginger, chilli and lime to give it flavour. I either grill it, or sometimes cook en papeot, which is wrapped in greaseproof paper. *Instead of* breadcrumbs for schnitzel or fried plaice (fish), I use quinoa flakes and add garlic pepper and dried chilli for seasonings.

Homemade Sauces etc

This page was created due to requests from members from our Ménière's disease group. Also, check out Low-sodium Foods Australia online to see what low-sodium sauces they have. Thanks to those who gave us recipes.

Worcestershire Sauce No-Added Salt
500mL malt vinegar, 1 teaspoon cayenne pepper, 4 teaspoons ground cloves, ¼ teaspoon allspice, ½ teaspoon mace, ½ teaspoon ginger, 1 clove crushed garlic, 1½ tablespoons brown sugar, 1 ½ tablespoons treacle, ¼ cup cold water. Mix all ingredients together, except the vinegar. Bring vinegar to the boil and add the other mixed ingredients. Simmer for 1 hour. Use cheesecloth to filter the liquid to exclude any sediment, then pour it into a bottle.

Vinaigrette No-Salt
½ cup red wine vinegar, ⅓ cup olive oil, 1 tablespoon Italian seasoning, 2 cloves garlic, crushed, 1 teaspoon lemon juice, ⅛ teaspoon white pepper. Mix together.

Homemade Sodium-free Soy Sauce
1½ cups of water, ¼ cup balsamic vinegar, 2 tablespoons apple cider vinegar, ¼ cup molasses, 1 teaspoon garlic powder, 1 teaspoon onion powder, ¼ teaspoon ground ginger, ¼ teaspoon ground black pepper. In a small saucepan, combine all ingredients. Bring to boil over a medium high heat. Reduce heat to low and simmer to 10 minutes, stirring occasionally. To add more flavour, use any no added salt broth.

Low-sodium Satay Sauce
1 tablespoon low-sodium Worcestershire sauce, 1 tablespoon honey, 1 dessertspoon low-sodium crushed garlic, 1 teaspoon low-sodium curry powder, 4 tablespoons low-sodium peanut butter, 2 tablespoons low-sodium sweet chilli sauce, 3 teaspoons sugar. Mix all together and add equal parts water and cooking cream until texture is suitable to your taste. Brush over chicken skewers, pour over pasta, or use as a stir-fry sauce - *Kim*

Low-sodium Tomato Sauce

Saute 2 teaspoons olive oil, ½ small onion finely chopped and 1 clove garlic (finely chopped). Mix ½ cup *no-salt* added tomato paste, ½ cup water, ¼ cup pineapple or orange juice, 3 tablespoons white vinegar, 1 ½ teaspoon brown sugar, ½ teaspoon ground black pepper. Add to the pan and simmer 3 minutes, then blend and puree for 1 minute. Use within 2 weeks.

Stir-fry Sauce Low Sodium

2 teaspoons cornstarch, 1 tablespoon water, ¼ cup soy sauce substitute, 1 tablespoon salt-free tomato paste or salt-free ketchup, 2 teaspoons sugar, 1 tablespoon sesame oil, 2 teaspoons balsamic vinegar, ½ tsp red pepper flakes, 2 cloves of raw garlic, pressed or minced.

Semi Dried Tomatoes

Cut smaller tomatoes in half, and bigger ones into quarters. Place tomatoes in an oven for 1 hour on 100° C (fan forced) followed by 30 minutes on 70° C. Turn off oven and leave tray in oven until it is cool to touch. Can be stored in the fridge for a few days or if using olive oil for a few weeks. *Alternative seasonings* - sprinkled freshly cracked black pepper over the tomatoes prior to putting in the oven. Try fresh basil leaves. Use over ripe tomatoes for the most intense flavour ~ *Francoise*

And... Sour Cream Mayonnaise

1 cup sour cream, 1 tablespoon Dijon mustard, 1 teaspoon lemon juice, 1 teaspoon brown sugar or honey, 3 teaspoons olive, oil, a sprinkle of paprika, pepper to taste, or no-salt salt. Blend all ingredients except the oil which you slowly add. Blend on high for 1 minute. Stores for up to 7 days.

Aunty Jude's Perky Pumpkin Soup

serves: 4 **prep:** 15 minutes **cooking time:** 30 minutes

Aunty Jude is one of my best friends, and my Aunty. We unfortunately share the MD monster. She loves to cook, always experimenting with healthy recipes to help her lifestyle and also shares they with others. I was her flower girl when I was little and we share a love of dogs and family. She has a huge heart of gold and everyone loves her to bits ~ Kim

Ingredients

- 2 tablespoons of olive oil
- 2 tablespoons of salt-reduced butter
- 1 packet of *Perky Pumpkin & Chilli Spice Mix*
- 2 tablespoons of low-sodium chicken stock powder
- 1 onion finely chopped
- 2 potatoes chopped into small pieces
- 2 carrots chopped into small pieces
- 1 medium butternut pumpkin cut into small pieces
- 1 can of coconut cream - 400mL (optional)

Method

1. Heat 2 tablespoons of olive oil and 2 tablespoons of butter.
2. Slowly saute onions.
3. Add spice mix and vegetables. Stir and cook on medium heat to generously coat with flavour.
4. Add chicken stock and some water just to cover the mix.
5. Turn up the heat and cook until the vegetables are soft.
6. Remove from heat and mash and blend until smooth.
7. Add 1 can of coconut cream (optional, but delicious - alternatively use low-sodium sour cream).

Sally's Minestrone Soup

serves: 4 **prep:** 20 minutes **cooking time:** 45 minutes

This recipe is great for either evening meals, or lunch on a winter's day. And the next day, and the day after that! I use a pressure cooker, but the same can be achieved in a large regular pot, with a longer cooking time. I've listed the vegetables I like, but really you can add anything. My minestrone comes out different every time, because it depends on what I include ~ Sally

Ingredients

- half a packet of Italian soup mix - a combination of dried beans and lentils. Don't stress if they get very soft and are undetectable - they thicken the mixture beautifully
- 300g (but depends how much you like) of casserole style steak - cut into pieces of about 1cm. I prefer chuck (optional: leave out for vegetarian/vegan minestrone)
- 1 large onion, chopped
- 2 cloves garlic, crushed
- 1-2 sticks celery, chopped into pieces about 1cm
- 1 large carrot, cut into chunks or rings
- 1 large potato, cubed
- small sweet potato, cubed
- chunk of pumpkin, cubed
- other veggies as desired e.g. fennel, zucchini, parsnip, turnip, green beans
- 2 cans of chopped tomatoes
- 1 packet of beef or vegetable stock. I like the *Maggie Beer* brand, but *Nuttelex Veggie Stock* is also great
- no-alcohol red wine (optional)
- dash or three of *Kick Start Hot Chilli Sauce*. This is a great alternative to salt-laden substances such as Worcester Sauce, Vegemite etc to give the dish a "lift". Start off using about a teaspoon, and taste at each stage … this will tell you whether you want to add more
- 1-2 tablespoons olive oil
- water

Method

1. Prepare veggies by using a saucepan with a steamer. Steam your prepared veggies until firm when a fork is inserted. I usually do this in batches as different veggies require different lengths of time. It is easy to end up with a mush instead of distinct chunks of veges. I am not confident enough to know when to add each veggie individually to cook within the mix and have found this method works. *Set the veggies aside.*
2. Heat olive oil in pressure cooker, or soup pot (large saucepan).
3. Add chopped onion and cook for about a minute.

4. Add meat to brown. Stir so that all sides are browned. Don't overcook.
5. Add crushed or chopped garlic and stir through.
6. Place liquids - stock, tinned tomatoes, hot chilli sauce, wine and a cup of water in pot.
   If using a pressure cooker - cover and set on to high for 10 minutes.
   If using a pot - cover and cook on a low setting until the beef is not quite tender.
7. Add the Italian soup Mix - about half a packet is sufficient.
   If using a pressure cooker - after adding dry soup mix, check liquid level, and add more water if necessary. Cover again and set to high for a further 10 minutes.
   If using a pot - check liquid level, cover again and cook further until the mix is tender.
8. When you are sure that the soup is to your taste, add all the steamed veggies and mix through. Leave on the stove long enough to finish off to the taste you like.

N.B. Tastes even richer the next day!

Gluepot Lentil and Pumpkin Soup

serves: 4 **prep:** 20 minutes **cooking time:** 45 minutes

This recipe is from Francoise, and she said it came from a camp at Gluepot Reserve, hence the name. Gluepot Reserve is in South Australia, and George Negus said it's "one of the conservation miracles of the 21st century".

Ingredients

- 1 large carrot chopped
- 1 large onion chopped
- 2 celery sticks - chopped
- ¾ cup red lentils
- 400g pumpkin - chopped
- 2 teaspoons ground coriander
- 2 teaspoon ground cumin
- 1 tablespoon finely chopped fresh ginger
- 1.5L water
- 1 x 440g tin no-added salt chopped tomatoes
- 2 tablespoons no added salt tomato paste
- juice of 1 lemon
- ½ cup pasta risoni
- 1 stick of cinnamon

Variations

- Omit carrot and add large chopped kumara and 150-200g pumpkin.
- Instead of red lentils, use 1 cup yellow split peas, rinsed.
- Add 1 teaspoon ground turmeric and ½ teaspoon cinnamon to the other spices.
- Add kernels of 2 large corn and add in the last 5 minutes of cooking.
- Add 330mL can of coconut milk at the end of cooking.

Serve with cornbread muffins.

Method

1. Check lentils for any foreign material e.g. rocks and remove.
2. Cook carrots, onion and celery for 10 minutes, stirring often.
3. Stir in pumpkin and stir for 1 minute. Add in coriander, cumin and ginger and stir for 1-2 minutes.
4. Add lentils, water, tomatoes and tomato paste. Stir and bring to boil. Reduce heat simmer for 20 minutes.
5. Check if lentils are cooked, if not, cook a further 5 minutes and check again.
6. Remove cinnamon stick before you blend the soup.
7. Add in the lemon juice.

Notes: If you want to keep some of soup for another day, don't add the risoni, but cook separately and add at the end of cooking the soup. The pasta will get very soft if left overnight.

Chicken & Veggie Soup

serves: 6 **prep:** 15 minutes **cooking time:** 45 minutes

This recipe reminds me of the smell of grandma's kitchen, there was something always on the stove or in the oven cooking, meals appeared easily and were always nutritious and yummy - Kim

Ingredients

- 2 tablespoons olive oil
- 1 leek, halved and thinly sliced
- 2 cloves garlic, crushed
- 1 carrot, diced
- 2 celery sticks, diced
- 1 zucchini, diced
- 1 swede, diced
- 1¼ cup of dry soup mix
- 1kg chicken pieces
- 10 cups water + 10 teaspoons of *Salt Skip* Chicken Stock, or you can use 5 x 500mL *The Stock Merchant Chicken Stock* (no-added salt)
- frozen or no-added salt canned corn
- drizzle of sesame oil

Method

1. Fry leek and garlic in oil until soft.
2. Add carrot, celery, zucchini, swede and fry until softened.
3. Add water and stock powder (or liquid stock) and dry soup mix. Cook for 15 minutes to heat stock up, then add chicken pieces.
4. Cook until chicken is cooked through.
5. Remove from stock and remove the meat and add the meat back to the soup.
6. Cook on a simmer for a couple of hours, adding the sesame oil and corn kernels 15 minutes before serving.

Serve and enjoy.

* Freezes well
* Makes a large amount

Chicken

Chicken with Ras el hanout

serves: 2-4 **prep:** 5 minutes **cooking time:** 15 minutes

Years ago, I encountered Golden Ras al Hanout, a North African spice mix. How delighted I was post-diagnosis to read the list of ingredients to find the brand I was using is sodium-free! ~ Sally

Ingredients

- 2 whole chicken breasts cut in halves horizontally, or 4 chicken breast schnitzels
- olive oil - about 2 tablespoons
- ras el hanout (a spice mix) - about a heaped teaspoon

Method

1. In a container, mix olive oil and ras el hanout so that it covers the surfaces of the chicken.
2. Place in a heavy based pan or wok, and drizzle the remainder of the olive oil from the container over.
3. Cook on a high heat until sizzling then lower heat until chicken is cooked through.

I love it served with roasted carrot chunks and steamed green beans.

Chicken and Mushroom Risotto

serves: 3-4 **prep:** 20 minutes **cooking time:** 35-40 minutes

Risotto has always been a favourite meal. While traditionally salt provides some "pep" to the taste, I have found substituting the hot chilli sauce in moderation provides a taste 'oomph' ~ Sally

Ingredients

- 1 cup Arborio rice
- 2 - 3 boned chicken thighs (you can use breast fillets, but thighs result in a richer taste) cut into small pieces - trim most of the fat off if you like, but leave some to create richness
- 1 -2 cups sliced button mushrooms
- 1 onion, diced
- 1-2 cloves garlic, crushed
- about 4-5 cups chicken stock, heated. I sometimes make my own stock by using chicken bones from a previous meal, or use a commercial low-sodium chicken stock, such as *Maggie Beer* Chicken Stock (96mg/100g sodium)
- *Kick Start Hot Chilli Sauce* - a couple of dashes. Start conservatively, taste and if you like more "zing", add more
- about a tablespoon of olive oil
- 100g unsalted butter
- optional - a tablespoon of nutritional yeast flakes as a substitute to cheese
- optional - cup of zero/low alcohol white wine if your Ménière's is affected by alcohol

Method

1. Heat olive oil and butter in a pan.
2. In a separate saucepan heat the stock until it comes to a boil. You can turn it off and add a lid at this point.
3. Add chicken and stir fry until browned on a moderate heat. Remove the chicken (this step is traditional, but I sometimes just leave it and keep adding the rest of the ingredients).
4. Add onion and stir until onion softens, add garlic and cook a further minute. Be careful not to burn the garlic.
5. Add the rice and make sure it is well coated with the oil and butter. If you like more butter, you can add a bit more.
6. Add the mushrooms.

7. Now start adding the stock, and wine if you are using it. Add a ladle at a time and stir the rice as you add the liquid. The trick is that the rice absorbs the liquid. *At this time* you should also add a bit of the hot chilli sauce. Not too much - but taste and see if it is to your taste. My household likes a bit of zing, to make up for no-salt.

8. As the liquid steams off, add more at intervals of about 30-40 seconds, making sure to stir each time. You need to watch it cook to make sure the liquid doesn't all disappear. If the stock and wine is not enough, top up with small amounts of water.

The correct texture for the risotto should be cooked through but not mush… just 'al dente' is perfect.

Before serving, or once in a bowl, stir in some nutritional yeast. Other family members who are not sodium-restricted may prefer *freshly grated parmesan* or *pecorino cheese*. This gives an added creaminess to the risotto.

Variations
- We sometimes add a cup of frozen peas
- And occasionally I make a puree of roasted pumpkin to make the stock

Fakeaway Nights - Honey Chicken

serves: 2 **prep:** 10 minutes **cooking time:** 30 minutes

I created this recipe after always being jealous of not being able to eat Chinese food when dining out. It's now a regular on our menu at home. Hubby says, 'It's better than the Chinese food shop!' (plus you know exactly what's in it) ~ Kim

Ingredients

- 1 chicken breast
- cornflour to dust the chicken in
- frozen stir-fry veggies, or add fresh if you prefer
- sesame seeds
- rice or noodles to serve

Sauce ingredients ...
• approximately 4 tablespoons of honey
• approximately 1 tablespoon of *Chilli Harvest Thai Sweet Chilli Sauce*

Method

1. Dice chicken breast into cubes.
2. Dust in cornflour to coat (this makes a crunchy coating).
3. Pan fry the diced chicken in oil until cooked and golden brown.
4. Add some stir-fry veggies.
5. At the same time, in a separate pan, I pan fried some sesame seeds until they just started to turn golden for the garnish.
6. When all the veggies are cooked, drizzle the sauce over and served it with rice or noodles, or you can keep the chicken separate and toss the chicken in the sauce by itself before adding back with the veggies.

To make the sauce...
Combine sauce ingredients, adding honey to your taste buds liking. Warm. *Double the sauce ingredients if you like lots of sauce.*

Chicken Sausage Rolls

Serves: 4-6 **prep:** 10minutes **cooking time:** 20 minutes

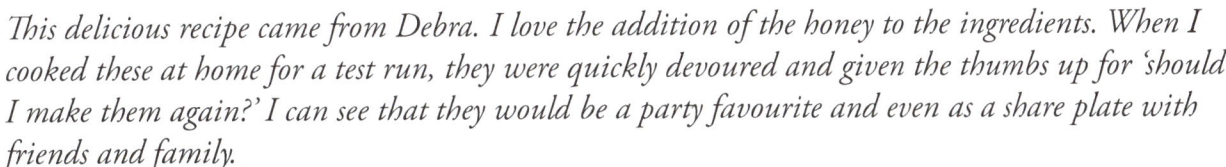

This delicious recipe came from Debra. I love the addition of the honey to the ingredients. When I cooked these at home for a test run, they were quickly devoured and given the thumbs up for 'should I make them again?' I can see that they would be a party favourite and even as a share plate with friends and family.

Ingredients

- 500g of chicken mince
- 2 tablespoons of honey
- 1 carrot grated
- 1 zucchini grated
- 1 onion chopped finely
- add any other vegetables you prefer to add to your mince
- Pampas butter puff pastry
- 1 sheet per recipe

Method

1. Combine mince vegetables and honey together.
2. Take a pastry sheet out of the freezer and place on tray to thaw. Cut in half.
3. Take half of mixture and place even amounts on each pastry sheet. Roll up sides.
4. Place into oven on 220º C for 20 minutes or until brown.

I serve mine with tomato relish from Quincy Jones Jelly 10mg per 100 grams. I usually place the extra half of mince tray in freezer for easy meal next time.

Sweet Chilli Chicken Rice

serves: 4-6 **prep:** 10 minutes **cooking time:** 15 minutes

Kim sent in this recipe for us and it certainly is very moorish. Sweet chilli chicken can be traced back to Asian cuisine (a blend of Chinese and Thai influence) and it now has become a popular, delightful dish, adapted to the tastes of where is it cooked. You can change it up with noodles or cauliflower rice, if you wish.

Ingredients

- sesame oil
- 500g diced chicken breast
- 4 tablespoons Sweet Chilli Sauce (low sodium) or to taste
- sliced: bok choy, carrot, capsicum, mushrooms, or vegetables of choice
- no-added salt corn kernels
- rice (microwave packet - or cook your own)

Method

1. In wok, pan fry chicken breast in oil until golden brown.
2. Add vegetables, cook until tender.
3. Add sweet chilli sauce and rice to pan and stir until combined & hot.
4. Enjoy.

Cantonese Chicken

serves: 4 **prep:** 15 minutes **cooking time:** 15 minutes

This recipe was generously donated by Anne. I think it hits the spot of those of us who loved to eat Chinese food before we were diagnosed with Ménière's, where we then didn't have to watch everything we ate.

Ingredients

- 2 tablespoons vegetable oil
- ½ onion, chopped
- 115g mushrooms, sliced
- 1 cup bok choy, chopped
- ¼ teaspoon ground ginger
- ¼ teaspoon garlic powder (or 1-2 cloves of garlic, crushed)
- ¼ tablespoon black pepper
- 2 chicken breasts, sliced thinly
- 1 tablespoon sherry
- 1 tablespoon *Maleny* or *Chilli Harvest Sweet Chilli Sauce*
- 1 cup of *Salt Skip* chicken stock
- 1 tablespoon cornflour
- 1 cup carrot, sliced

Method

1. In a wok heat half the oil.
2. Add the carrot, onion and half the spices. Stir fry for 2 minutes.
3. Add mushrooms and bok choy. Stir fry for another minute.
4. Remove vegetables from wok.
5. Heat remaining oil and then add chicken and remaining spices and stir fry until chicken is no longer pink.
6. Return all the vegetables to the wok.
7. Mix together the chilli sauce, sherry, chicken stock and cornflour. Add to wok and heat until mixture thickens and begins to bubble.

Photo shows Cantonese Chicken with the bok choy whole, and an added egg (optional)

Chicken Vadouvan Recipe

serves: 6 **prep:** 15 minutes **cooking time:** 40 minutes

Vadouvan Curry is an Indian east coast curry inspired by French colonists. The French who colonized the Pondicherry area of eastern India took a liking to the local flavours and made this version their own. A larger-than-usual leaning towards dried onion and garlic, and the freshness of curry leaves, makes this blend mild and a little sweet ~ Anne

Ingredients

- 2 tablespoons oil
- 1 onion, finely chopped
- 2 tablespoons Vadouvan curry mix
- juice of 1 lemon, or 1 teaspoon tamarind paste
- 600g chicken breast or thighs, cubed
- 1 cup plain yoghurt
- coriander leaves to serve

Method

1. Fry onion in oil in a large pan.
2. Add curry powder and stir for 1 minute.
3. Add chicken and stir to seal on all sides.
4. Add sufficient water to just cover chicken.
5. Add lemon juice or tamarind paste.
6. Simmer for 20 minutes or until meat is cooked through.
7. Remove from heat and stir in yoghurt.

Serve with rice, garnishing with coriander leaves.

Butter Chicken

serves: 6 **prep:** 25 minutes **cooking time:** 1 hour

Butter Chicken is a classic Indian dish which originated in Northern India, more specifically, in Delhi in the 1950s. Anne has given us this recipe, which she adapted, based on Herbie's Butter Chicken Seasoning. It's a dish of spiced chicken in a creamy tomato sauce, and pairs beautifully with rice and homemade naan bread.

Ingredients

- 1kg of chicken, chopped into large bite size pieces - use breast, thighs or tenderloins, as you prefer
- 1 packet *Herbie's Butter Chicken Seasoning**
- 1 tablespoon butter or olive oil
- 375g approximately of plain yoghurt
- 1 tablespoon of crushed garlic
- 1 medium onion finely diced or pureed
- 2 tablespoons of low-salt tomato sauce (*Pops*)
- 1 tablespoon of brown sugar
- 1 tablespoon of low-salt tomato paste
- 1 tablespoon of *Chilli Harvest Mild Mango Chutney*
- 1 tablespoon of ground almonds
- 200mL single or cooking cream
- 1 small can of coconut milk (approximately 85 to 100mL)
- 1 tablespoon of chopped coriander leaves or a pinch of dried coriander.

* Available at Low-Sodium Foods Australia

Method

1. Mix the chicken pieces with half the *Herbie's Butter Chicken Seasoning* combined with the yoghurt. **Cover and marinate overnight in the refrigerator.**
2. Next day, add oil, garlic and onion to a heavy pan and fry for 2-3 minutes.
3. Remove chicken pieces from marinade (there will be very little marinade left in bowl) and add to onion and garlic mixture. Cook chicken on high for 5-10 minutes.
4. Add coconut milk, tomato sauce, tomato paste, sugar, coriander, almonds, mango chutney and any remaining marinade to the pan with the chicken mixture. Stir well.
5. Bring to simmer temperature and cook covered for 45 minutes or until you are satisfied chicken is tender and flavoursome.
6. When ready to serve, add cream and reheat mixture.

Apricot Chicken – 4 Ways

serves: 4-6 **prep:** 15 minutes **cooking time:** varies with recipe

When we put the callout for recipes for the Ménière's disease cookbook, we expected maybe one of Apricot Chicken, but four recipes came in, so we have added them all here. We hope that one of the recipes suits your tastebuds.

Apricot Chicken 1 - Ingredients

- 1 can apricot nectar
- 2-3 tablespoons *Masterfoods No Added Salt All Purpose Blend*
- 1 onion, finely sliced
- 1 cup of chopped dried apricots (optional)
- 500g chicken drumsticks, wings or sliced chicken fillets

1 - Method
Kim

1. Lay chicken pieces in casserole dish.
2. Combine all other ingredients in bowl and pour over chicken.
3. Cook for approximately 45 minutes 180º C (depending on cut of meat).

Serve with rice, and vegetables. Enjoy.

Apricot Chicken 2 - Ingredients

- 500g chicken breast chopped into bite size pieces
- 1 stick celery chopped
- 1 x 415g tin pie apricot or apricots
- 1 tablespoon grated fresh ginger
- 400mL apricot nectar
- ½ teaspoon five spice powder
- ½ cup medium dry sherry
- 1 teaspoon corn flour
- 1 large spanish onion sliced

2 - Method
Francoise

1. Cook chicken pieces in a tablespoon of olive oil, until golden brown or cooked. Then remove chicken pieces from the pan and put aside.
2. Sauté onions and celery in a small amount of olive oil until onions are almost translucent or soft.
3. Add sherry and simmer gently for a few minutes.
4. Add grated ginger and stir in.
5. Add the apricot puree and most of the apricot juice (leave some aside to mix in cornflour) and heat until it boils.
6. Reduce heat. Add and stir in the five spice powder. Add the cooked chicken and re-heat for a further few minutes.
7. If mixture is a little watery then mix cornflour in with left over apricot nectar. Cook for a further few minutes until mixture thickens.

Serve with white rice and vegetables such as carrots, beans or broccoli.

Apricot Chicken - 4 Ways

serves: 4-6 **prep:** 15 minutes **cooking time:** varies

Apricot Chicken 3 - Ingredients

- 1 x 825g can tinned apricots in juice (less than 125mg/100g sodium)
- 1 x 405g tin apricot nectar
- 4 x chicken whole skinned chicken breasts
- very small amount of plain flour
- ground black pepper
- olive oil
- 1 red onion
- garlic to taste (I use about 3 cloves)
- chives

Serving
I like to serve this with steamed carrots and an ancient grains mix. For that I prefer Coles Nutritious 7 Ancient Grains blend, which is heated in a microwave for 90 seconds. it has 42mg/100g sodium.

3 - Method
Sally

1. Preheat oven to 200º C.
2. Chop onion and crush garlic.
3. Brush the chicken breasts with a light dusting of flour. You don't need very much. Too much will make the dish too gluggy.
4. Heat about 2 tablespoons of olive oil in an oven-proof dish, on the stove top.
5. Brown the chicken breasts in the pan and remove. Add onion and garlic (you can add more olive oil if needed), and cook gently until soft.
6. Add chicken, apricots and apricot nectar, as well as a few twists of black pepper to the oven-proof dish.
7. Cover and bake for about 30 minutes, or until chicken is cooked and tender. The apricot should have formed a lovely spoonable sauce, and the apricot halves should still be intact.

Apricot Chicken 4 - Ingredients

Preheat oven to 180º C
- 410g can apricot nectar
- 4 chicken thighs
- 1 egg
- flour to coat chicken
- 1 packet salt-reduced french onion soup

4 - Method
Julieann

1. Coat chicken thighs in egg, then flour, then egg again and fry until golden brown.
2. Mix apricot nectar and french onion soup in a casserole dish, then add the fried chicken and place the lid on the dish.
3. Cook in a 180º C oven for 1 hour.

Serve with rice, and/or vegetables. Enjoy.

Chicken Wraps

serves: 4-6 **prep:** 15 minutes **cooking time:** 1 hour

Chicken Wraps are always a favourite with my family. All three of my kids eat it (usually one of them doesn't like what we're eating, and have to make their own dinner - that's the rule). We love to load up the wraps with lots of salad, and there is also sour cream on the table to add ~ Julieann

Ingredients

- 4 chicken thighs
- BBQ sauce - salt-reduced
- lettuce
- tomato - sliced or diced
- low-salt cheese - grated
- avocado - sliced
- carrot - grated
- Wraps - *Simson's Pantry* - lite low carb super grains has the lowest salt, but choose a tortilla or wrap that you know is okay for you.

For a bit of variety, instead of BBQ sauce, use a low-sodium sauce that you like. We also coat the chicken in Sweet Chilli Sauce instead of the BBQ sauce. Tastes delish!

Method

1. Preheat the oven to 180º C.
2. Place the chicken thighs in a baking dish and coat with BBQ sauce to your liking.
3. Place in the oven for an hour, turning every 20 minutes.
4. Meanwhile, prepare the salad ingredients and place on a large plate or wooden board for serving.
5. When the chicken is cooked, slice up into small pieces and place onto the large plate/wooden board, and add to the table for family or friends to construct their own chicken wrap.

We also add condiments to the table such as mayonnaise, sweet chilli sauce, Greek yoghurt, sour cream light etc. for individual taste preferences.

Crumbed Chicken Fillets with Capsicum Sauce

serves: 4-6 **prep:** 15 minutes **cooking time:** 45 minutes or less

This recipe came from Wendy. It is interesting to note that according to research, no one can agree on where the method of crumbed chicken came from. Was it Scotland? The American South? The Italians? Germany or Switzerland? I'm settling for the Scottish and West Africans.

Ingredients

Crumbed chicken

- 4-6 chicken thigh fillets trimmed of excess fat and cut each into 2-3 pieces depending on size.
- 2 tablespoons of gluten-free flour (I use chickpea)
- gluten-free *Gourmet Thai* Sweet Chilli Sauce
- ½ cup gluten free dried breadcrumbs (or 2 tablespoons of almond meal and a couple of good handfuls of crushed gluten free Cornflakes)

Method

1. Place into a plastic bag.
2. Add gluten-free flour and shake the bag to evenly coat chicken.
3. Add gluten-free "Gourmet Thai" Sweet Chilli sauce and gently massage to coat chicken.
4. Add ½ cup gluten-free dried breadcrumbs and gently shake to thoroughly coat (or 2 tablespoons of almond meal and a couple of good handfuls of crushed gluten-free Cornflakes).
5. Cook crumbed fillets over medium heat in a non-stick fry pan till golden and cooked through (or use baking paper to line a fry pan).

Ingredients

Capsicum Sauce

- 1 large red capsicum
- 1 tablespoon unsalted butter
- 2 tablespoons no-added salt tomato sauce
- 1 tablespoon brown sugar
- 80-90mL cream (or sour cream)

Method

1. Blitz all except cream in a food processor until fairly smooth.
2. Cook over medium heat, simmering for around 8-10 minutes till slightly thickened, add cream and heat through.

Serve over chicken.

Beef, Lamb, Pork

Sally's Pasta Ragu (aka Spag Bol)

serves: 4 **prep:** 20 minutes **cooking time:** 1 hour 20 minutes

This bolognaise inspired ragù owes a debt to my Sicilian mother-in-law. You can use any type of pasta; my favourite is spaghetti or linguine, but shorter forms like penne are fine too. While this recipe does use some milk, those with Coeliac issues should not be put off - you can omit it and add another cup of stock or tomato ~ Sally

Ingredients

- 500g of mixed beef and pork mince
- 1 medium or large onion - white or red, chopped into small pieces
- 1 large stalk of celery, finely chopped
- 1 medium carrot, grated or chopped in food processor
- 2 (or more depending on taste) cloves garlic, finely sliced or crushed
- olive oil - about a tablespoon, more to taste.
- 1 x 400g tin of diced tomatoes - there are several brands available with sodium about 10mg/100g
- 1 - 2 cups of beef stock - I use *Maggie Beer Natural Beef Stock* 93mg/100g sodium
- 1 - 2 cups of tomato passata - I use *Australian Organic Food Co Classic Tomato Passata* 21mg/100g sodium)
- 2 tablespoon low-sodium tomato paste
- 1 cup milk
- A couple of splashes of hot chilli sauce - I use *Kick Start*. This adds a depth that many salt eaters say the recipe doesn't otherwise provide. Over time you will experiment with how much you like.

Method

1. A first step in any ragù is to make a soffritto - a base comprising onions, celery, carrot and garlic.
2. Heat olive oil in a heavy-based pan.
3. Add onions, carrot, celery, garlic. I don't bother doing them separately.
4. Cook in the olive oil until soft.
5. Add mince and cook until browned.
6. Add diced tomatoes, beef stock, passata, milk, chilli sauce and tomato paste.
7. Allow to simmer for a minimum of an hour, longer will not hurt it. Top up with liquids if you feel they are needed.

Always tastes better the next day! Freezes well.

Slow Cooked Lamb Shanks

serves: 2 **prep:** 20 minutes **cooking time:** 8 hours slow cooker

We have the most amazing butcher shop here in our small community, and Mallee lamb is the pride of the place - so lamb shanks are of course delicious however they're cooked. But when slow cooked they fall off the bone and melt in your mouth. Absolutely delicious! Try them slow cooked. You'll thank me ~ Kim

Ingredients

- 2 lamb shanks
- 1 can chopped tomatoes
- 1 onion, chopped or sliced
- 1 teaspoon crushed garlic
- 1 tablespoon mixed herbs
- 2 cups beef stock
- splash of red wine (optional)
- 500g mushrooms, sliced
- 1 carrot, sliced
- cornflour to thicken (make slurry with water)

Method

1. In bowl of slow cooker add all ingredients except cornflour slurry.
2. Slow cook for 8 hours on low.
3. Once cooked, remove shanks and thicken sauce with cornflour, cook for 2 minutes, then pour sauce over shanks.

Serve with mashed potatoes or vegetables of your choice.

Italian Lamb with Balsamic Glaze

serves: 4 **prep:** 5 minutes **cooking time:** 2 hours 30 minutes

An Italian colleague of my husband gave him this recipe, and I adapted it to suit. With the price increases in lamb in recent times, it has become a "special occasion" dish ~ Sally

Ingredients

1 x boned and trimmed leg of lamb

Marinade

- ½ cup extra virgin olive oil
- 2 sprigs fresh rosemary
- 2 crushed cloves of garlic
- freshly ground black pepper

Glaze

- ¼ cup balsamic vinegar
- ¼ cup olive oil
- 2 tablespoons brown sugar

Method

1. Preheat oven to 180º C (fan forced).
2. Warm the marinade ingredients gently together.
3. Pour over the lamb.
4. *Marinate overnight.*
5. Cook the lamb in an oven proof baking dish, on a rack, with a packet of beef stock in the base of the pan. You can add water as you go if it dries out. This and the lamb juices are great for making a gravy at the end.

   I generally cook on both sides for about 10 minutes and then turn the oven down to 160º C, and cook for a minimum of 2 hours so that it is very, very tender.
6. Mix the glaze ingredients together to dissolve the sugar.
7. Brush on the glaze in the last 10 minutes of cooking.

Shepherd's Pie

serves: 4-6 **prep:** 20 minutes **cooking time:** 60 minutes

This recipe came from Ruth. It's certainly a hearty dinner loved over many generations. Originally from the United Kingdom in the late 18th century, is was created to use up leftover roast meat. It's called Shepherd's pie because it traditionally uses lamb, associated with sheep herded by shepherds.

Ingredients

- 500g lamb mince
- 1 very finely chopped onion
- 1 medium carrot, grated
- 1 finely cut pear or apple (peeled and cored)
- 3 teaspoons no-added salt Worcestershire sauce
- ½ teaspoon *Keens Mustard powder*
- 1 teaspoon no-added salt garlic from a jar
- ½ cup Heinz salt-reduced tomato soup concentrate
- ½ cup no-added salt chutney (any variety)
- 1½ teaspoons no-added salt mild curry powder
- mashed potato for the topping

Method

1. Preheat oven to 200° C.
2. Heat oil in a large saucepan (medium heat).
3. Add onion, carrot and pear or apple and cook until soft.
4. Add lamb mince, until lamb changes colour, breaking up any lumps.
5. Add Worcestershire sauce, keens mustard powder, garlic, tomato soup concentrate, chutney, and curry and stir well.
6. Bring to the boil, reduce heat to low and cook for 30 minutes, stirring occasionally.
7. Spoon mixture into a large oven-proof baking dish and top with mashed potato - top with mashed potato, sprinkle with Macro brand Nutritional Yeast flakes (optional).
8. Bake in oven for around 20 minutes until potato is golden brown.

We also add condiments to the table such as mayonnaise, sweet chilli sauce, Greek yoghurt, sour cream light etc. for individual taste preferences.

Beef Nachos

serves: 6 **prep:** 15 minutes ***cooking time:*** *30 minutes or less*

This is one of my family's favs. My poor suffering children, who have never had salt added to their homemade food because their mum hated having 4 hour violent vertigo attacks. Love the flavour in this dish - Julieann

Ingredients

- 500g beef mince
- onion - diced
- Taco Spice Mix - *Old El Paso* reduced-salt (or make your own taco spice mix - below)
- ½ cup low-salt tomato sauce
- ½ cup water
- red kidney beans (low-salt)
- 2 tablespoons brown sugar
- ½ capsicum - diced
- lettuce
- tomato - diced
- low-salt cheese - grated
- avocado - mashed
- corn chips - low-salt
- sour cream light

Homemade no-salt taco spice mix

1 tablespoon cumin, 1 tablespoon ground chilli powder, ½ teaspoon cayenne pepper, 1 teaspoon onion powder and garlic powder, 1 teaspoon dried oregano, ¼ teaspoon smoked paprika, black pepper to taste (¼ teaspoon or less). Mix it all together.

Method

To make the Beef Mix

1. Add 1 tablespoon of olive oil to a saucepan and heat.
2. Add the diced onions and cook until they are transparent.
3. Add the beef mince and cook until it is brown.
4. Add the taco spice mix and stir, letting it infuse together for about a minute.
5. Add the low salt tomato sauce and water
6. Add the capsicum, red kidney beans and brown sugar.
7. Let the beef nacho mix cook on low heat for about 10 minutes.

Now for the nacho stack - Olé!

- Place low-salt corn chips on a plate - amount to your liking.
- Add the beef mix to your liking on top.
- Then add lettuce, tomato, cheese, mashed avocado, cheese and sour cream (optional)

Dig in and enjoy!

Instead of using corn chips, you can add the beef mix and salad to low-salt taco shells, or low-salt tortilla wraps. Sometimes we make it in to a taco bowl, and add rice mixed with low-salt black beans.

Calypso Beef

serves: 4-6 **prep:** 15 minutes **cooking time:** 35 minutes

This recipe came from Francoise. When I read the name of the recipe, my mind was immediately transported to Caribbean island life and rainforest reserves, bird sanctuaries and the vibrant turquoise water, and hearing the calypso style of music that originated in Trinidad.

Ingredients

- 500g round steak cut into bite size pieces
- 1 large onion roughly chopped
- 1 tablespoons of mixed herbs
- 1 clove garlic finely chopped
- 1 carrot sliced
- 2 teaspoons *Quincey Jones* Worcestershire Sauce
- 1 cup of water or stock
- 140g pack no-added salt tomato paste
- 440g tin of pineapple pieces (discard

Method

1. Fry in a little olive oil the onions, meat and mixed herbs until meat in browned and onion is softened.
2. Add garlic and fry a further minute.
3. Add the water or stock and simmer gently for about 10-15 minutes.
4. Add Worcestershire sauce.
5. Add carrot, and simmer gently until carrots are cooked.
6. Stir in tomato paste, then add the pineapple pieces but NOT the juice. Heat for about a minute then serve.
7. Serve with white rice and steamed broccoli or green beans.

Thai Salad – option to add your own meat

Ingredients

- angel hair pasta
- 1 can of water chestnuts, sliced
- 1 thinly julienned carrot
- 1 pk of baby corn sliced in half
- sliced snow peas
- 1 capsicum of choice, thinly sliced

Method

1. Cook angel hair pasta and cool.
2. Add other ingredients.
3. Add a cold low-salt meat of your choice.
4. Combine all in bowl and drizzle with *Maleny Thai Salad Dressing* and enjoy.

Sprinkle no added salt cashew nuts or peanuts on top.

Beef or Pork or Veal or Chicken Schnitz

serves: 4 **prep:** 15 minutes **cooking time:** *30 minutes or less*

My family are not KFC fans, but they do like homemade fried chicken. I also use this recipe and switch around the meat that is the schnitz. I have two versions of the crumbing chicken here. My fav is the parmi version ~ Julieann

Ingredients

- 4 pieces of thin sliced meat of your choice
- plain flour for coating, 2 large eggs
- 3-4 cups of homemade breadcrumbs
- 2 teaspoons cinnamon, 2 teaspoons black pepper, 4 teaspoons star anise - ground, pinch of medium heat chilli powder (optional) - similar to Chinese five-spice
- *or* ½ teaspoon thyme, ½ teaspoon basil, ⅓ teaspoon oregano, 1 teaspoon celery salt, 1 teaspoon black pepper, 1 teaspoon dried mustard, 4 teaspoons paprika, 2 teaspoons garlic salt, 1 teaspoon ground ginger, 3 teaspoons white pepper, 2 cups plain flour (*think KFC...*)
- olive oil for frying

Parmi Version Ingredients

- 4 chicken thighs
- 3-4 cups of homemade breadcrumbs
- 2 large eggs, no spices added

Topping
- SPC crushed tomatoes 400g (no-salt added)
- 2 tablespoons of no-added salt tomato paste
- 1 tablespoon of brown sugar
- 1 cube of reduced-salt beef stock
- thinly sliced less-salt ham
- Swiss cheese for the top

Method

1. Mix the eggs in a bowl.
2. Mix the breadcrumbs with the spice mix of your choice.
3. Dip the meat into the egg mixture, then the breadcrumb mixture (or the second option of flour & spices), and fry in a pan until golden.
4. Transfer the chicken to a tray lined with baking paper and pop it into an oven pre-heated to 180º C for around 20 minutes.

Serve with veggies or salad.

Parmi Version Method

1. Mix the eggs on a plate.
2. Mix the breadcrumbs and leave on a plate.
3. Dip the meat into the egg mixture, then the breadcrumb mixture, and fry in a pan until golden.
4. Transfer the meat to a tray lined with baking paper.
5. Mix together the tomatoes, tomato paste, brown sugar and beef stock cube and spread over the fried meat.
6. Top with a thin slice of the ham, then cheese.
7. Pop it into an oven pre-heated to 180º C for around 20 minutes.

Serve with veggies or salad (or on top of pasta to my horror! Or hot unsalted chips. I'll have to try it).

Greek Lamb and Salad

serves: 2 - 4 **prep:** 30 minutes **cooking time:** 50 minutes

What I love about this is… it's a fabulous, multi-purpose meal that's quick, nutritious, packed with wonderful flavours and there are no specific ingredient amounts. If the lack of specific recipe ingredients worries you, may be best to look away now. Easily adaptable to suit your own personal preference and requirements. Serve as main meal for lunch of dinner, it's great for picnics too. But wait, there's more… Grab a flat bread, fill it up with slices of lamb and salad, grill on sandwich maker for a delicious wrap full of flavour and goodness! ~ Libby

Lamb - Ingredients

- Lamb steaks x 4

Marinade
- juice of 2 to 3 lemons
- a little finely grated lemon zest
- olive oil – a good glug
- 4 smashed cloves of garlic
- oregano – fresh or dried to taste - I sprinkle herbs generously
- cracked black pepper

Salad - Ingredients

I use the following ingredients:
- lots of sliced cucumber for freshness and crunch
- handful of cherry tomatoes sliced in half
- thinly sliced red onion
- generous amount of feta cheese, your choice of marinated or natural (for the family). You can use goat cheese if you prefer it. I leave it out due to salt content, but my family loves it
- sprinkle of oregano – fresh or dried
- sometimes I throw in some washed Cos lettuce leaves as well
- a light splash of Balsamic or red wine vinegar, toss and serve
- some olives for the family - I take them out for me

I have just listed what I use as a guide, but the beauty is, it doesn't have to be exact, you just make it to suit your own taste.

My feta of choice comes from my local Farmers market and is marinated in lemon and garlic, it's rich and gooey and a truly incredible taste sensation.

Lamb - Method

1. Mix all ingredients together and pour over the lamb steaks.
2. Cover in glass bowl, refrigerate for minimum of 30 minutes if possible to tenderize and absorb flavours while you make the salad. The acidic lemon juice in the marinade aids in 'precooking process' and tenderizes the lamb plus adding a fresh, zesty flavour. Lamb steaks are generally quite thin so after marinating they only take less than 10 minutes in the oven to cook.
3. Remove steaks from marinade and cook on oven tray for 6 to 8 minutes on 170º C. Cooking time is dependent on your personal preference as to how you like your meat to be cooked and how thin or thick the lamb steaks are.

Salad - Method

Go nuts and make it however you like!

Side note: I know some people add capers, sliced radish, capsicum to their Greek salads. Just do your own thing with whatever you love using, making it visually gorgeous and delicious.
After all, apparently it was Apicius, the 1st Century Roman gourmand who purportedly coined the phrase, "We eat first with our eyes".

So, that's it, all that's left to do now is sit back and enjoy it, Cheers and good health, *Libby* (Ménière's warrior for 35 years and counting and quite possibly one of the world's worst cooks!)

Roast Pork with Beer Crispy Crackling

serves: 4 **prep:** 20 minutes **cooking time:** 2 hours

This is a German way of making a crispy crackling on a roast pork. I don't add salt to any of my dishes but spice it up with many other no-salt ingredients. This dish has no-salt included however naturally occurring salt within the pork or other ingredients may be present. I buy my pork from an organic butcher so there are no additives included, though I guess some butchers may sell pork where salt or preservatives are injected ~ Marion

Ingredients

- 2kg pork belly or shoulder with rind
- 1 onion - chopped
- 1 leek - chopped
- 2 carrots - chopped
- ½ bulb of garlic - crushed
- 1 teaspoon sweet paprika
- pepper
- 1 bottle 330mL - 500mL beer preferable - a Pils or lager

Method

1. Preheat oven to 180° C.
1. Pat the skin dry with paper towel.
2. Wash the vegetables, roughly chop them and place them with the garlic into the baking dish.
3. Rub the underside with paprika, and pepper.
4. Use a sharp knife to cut diamond-shaped cuts into the rind or ask the butcher to do it for you.
5. Place the pork with the flesh side in the baking dish (rind side up).
6. And add some water or *no-salt* vegetable stock in the base of the baking dish for about 30 minutes.
7. After 30 minutes increase the heat to 200° C and cook for another 1 hour and 30 minutes and poor beer over the roast every 20-30 minutes. If the roast is cooked but the rind not quite hard yet increase the heat for another 5-10 minutes.

Stroganoff Pork Meatballs

serves: 4-6 **prep:** 20 minutes **cooking time:** 1 hour or less

Wendy gave us this recipe. The name 'Stroganoff' in recipes comes from one of the members of the wealthy Stroganoff family, in Russia, back in the 1800s. They were aristocrats who hosted large 'open tables' where their French chefs would create dishes. The first recorded stroganoff recipe was a beef one, then variations of that recipe evolved.

Pork Meatballs

Ingredients

- 500g pork mince
- ½ leek finely chopped
- ½ red capsicum finely chopped
- ½ sachet quick oats
- 1 egg

Method

1. Preheat oven to 160º C.
2. Combine all together and roll into small meatballs and roll in plain flour (or gluten-free flour)
3. Brown the meatballs in 2 tablespoons of oil if you like, or simply place the raw meatballs in a single layer in a casserole dish.

Sauce

Ingredients

- 100g chopped button mushrooms
- ½ teaspoon allspice
- ½ teaspoon no-added salt curry powder
- ¼ teaspoon ground nutmeg
- 1 tablespoon gluten-free plain flour
- 1 sachet Legos no-added salt tomato paste
- 1 teaspoon grated fresh ginger
- 2 tablespoons white vinegar
- 1 tablespoon brown sugar
- a good grinding of black pepper
- 1½ cups no-added salt beef stock
- ¼ cup cooking cream
- a small handful of currants

Method

1. Mix all sauce ingredients, pour over meatballs. Cover.
2. Cook 160º C about 45-50 minutes or until cooked through and sauce has thickened.

Serve with steamed broccolini and crusty no added salt bread.

Pumpkin & Ricotta Lasagne

serves: 6 **prep:** 35 min **cooking time:** 35 minutes

Ruth sent us this recipe to include in our Ménière's Cookbook. I love the combination of flavours and the comfort that it brings. The recipe doesn't have a particular history, but it is a celebration of the modern fusion of blending ricotta (Italy) and lasagna (Italy) and adding pumpkin. It reminds me of Autumn and Winter vegetables.

Ingredients

- Instant lasagne sheets or 1 packet fresh pasta sheets (8)
- 1.2kg butternut pumpkin, skin removed and diced (or kent pumpkin)
- 30g butter
- 2 onions, diced
- 500g ricotta cheese
- ½ cup *low salt* sun-dried tomatoes, chopped
- ½ teaspoon nutmeg
- ¼ cup fresh parsley, chopped
- ¼ cup low-salt Parmesan cheese, grated
- 2 red capsicums, roasted and sliced
- pepper to taste

Add chopped walnuts if you like.

Method

1. Skin and dice the pumpkin and steam it until the pumpkin is soft.
2. In a large saucepan, cook the onion in the butter until golden.
3. Add the pumpkin, put the lid on the pot, and cook on a low heat for 5 minutes.
4. Spread a small amount of the pumpkin/onion mix over the base of a large baking dish so that the pasta sheets don't stick.
5. Cover it with a layer of pasta sheets.
6. Add a layer of a third of the pumpkin/onion mix, then a third of the ricotta cheese. Scatter some of the sun-dried tomatoes and nutmeg.
7. Add another layer of pasta sheets, then another third of the pumpkin/onion mix, and another third of the ricotta.
8. Top with slices of roasted capsicum and chopped parsley. Add another layer of pasta sheets, the rest of the pumpkin/onion mix and ricotta.
9. Grate the Parmesan cheese on top, and add pepper to taste (optional).
10. Put the lasagne into an oven preheated to 180° C for 25-35 minutes, or until the top is golden brown.

Serve with a side salad and crusty bread.

Vegetarian Mini Pizzas

serves: 2-4 **prep:** 15 minutes **cooking time:** up to 15 minutes

When Kim and Julieann met Sally online to discuss pizzas. We discovered that we used different pizza bases but still included them here. We discussed sodium content of sauces and discovered that Kim makes a chicken pizza with the satay sauce base as well. But this is the vegetarian one we decided on. Of course you can add your own ingredients or remove ingredients you don't like ~ Sally, Kim & Julieann

Ingredients

Pizza Base - *2 options*
No-salt pizza dough
- 2 cups of flour, 2 tablespoons of sugar, 2 ¼ teaspoons of yeast, 3 tablespoons of olive oil, up to ½ cup warm water
- or Nevana Pizza Bases (12 in the pack)

Base toppings
- no-added salt tomato paste - add a clove of crushed garlic and a dash of hot chilli sauce (optional)
- or pesto (p97)
- or satay sauce (p60)
- or Greek yoghurt

Topping
- capsicum
- onion
- pineapple
- mushrooms
- spring onions
- sun dried tomato
- topped with baby bocconcini
- a sprinkle of mixed herbs
- drizzle of Thai sweet chilli sauce
- or roasted vegetables, adding a sprinkle of thyme and rosemary

Throw some baby spinach, or basil, or rocket or kale etc on top if you like.

Method

Pizza base
1. Add all dough ingredients with a spatula, adding more flour if the dough is too sticky.
2. Grease a large bowl and put the dough into it. Cover with cling wrap and let the dough rise for about 30 minutes.
3. Flour a work surface to knead the dough and then make your pizza base. Makes 2 large pizzas.
4. Or use Nevana pizza bases.

Preheat oven 220º C.
1. On top of the pizza base, spread the tomato paste or pesto or satay sauce topping evenly.
2. Throw on your topping choices.
3. If using the *pre-prepared* pizza base, cook in the oven for around 15 minutes.
4. If *making your own pizza dough*, bake for 7-10 minutes or until the pastry is crusty.

Serve the pizzas on their own, or add a salad on the side.

Vegan Pesto

serves: 2-4 **prep:** 15 minutes **cooking time:** 0 minutes

I saw Vegan Pesto, similar to this in a cookbook, and tweaked it to include the nutritional yeast. My hairdresser introduced me to nutritional yeast flakes as an alternative to parmesan. Thanks Brigitte!
~ Sally

Ingredients

- ¾ cup of lightly toasted pine nuts
- ⅓ cup of freshly squeezed lemon juice
- clove of garlic, or two if you love garlic
- ground black pepper
- 3-4 cups of fresh basil leaves
- about ½ cup of olive oil - the best quality you can afford - try for extra virgin olive oil. If you use more, you will get a smoother pesto
- 1½ -2 tablespoons of nutritional yeast. There are several brands available. I use *Natural Nutritional Yeast Flakes* by *Honest to Goodness*. The sodium content is 60mg/100g

Method

1. Combine pine nuts, lemon juice, garlic and pepper in the food processor and chop them well.
2. Add the basil, and keep going until combined. Depending on the size of your food processor (I have a small one), you may need to add in batches.
3. Drizzle the olive oil in a bit at a time and mix until combined to a smooth paste.
4. Last step, add the nutritional yeast.

Your pesto is now ready to use, preferably with long flat pasta like linguine, to which it clings the best. You can store it in the fridge for a week or so. In that case I recommend putting a few millimetres of olive oil over the top of it in a jar.

Brown Rice and Tuna Salad

serves: 3-4 **prep:** 15 minutes **cooking time:** up to 40 minutes

This recipe was sent in by Francoise. It has no added salt tuna as one of the ingredients, which will surprise some people are they associate salt with tuna. The lovely combination of cherry tomatoes, cucumber and rocket leaves creates a fresh and satisfying flavour on your palate. Change it up by using a different salad dressing if you like, or experiment with a rice of your choosing.

Ingredients

- 1⅓ cups brown rice
- approximately ½ cup *Praise* Balsamic & Garlic dressing, or to taste
- 200g punnet cherry tomatoes, halved
- 2 Lebanese cucumber, diced
- 50g baby rocket leaves
- 425g no-added salt tuna

Method

1. Cook rice and drain well.
2. Set aside to cool for 5 minutes.
3. Stir through dressing.
4. Set aside for 15 minutes.
5. Add all other ingredients, season with pepper and gently toss to combine.

Prawn and Mussel Pasta Sauce

serves: 3-4 **prep:** 5 minutes **cooking time:** 25 minutes

This is a quick and easy meal, which I love. This quantity should feed 3 or 4 people, or two with some leftovers! ~ Sally

Ingredients

- Spaghetti for the number of people eating
  I think this is best suited to a traditional spaghetti rather than shorter pastas like penne. But that is up to your preference.
- frozen prawns - 1 packet - I have trawled through the freezers at various supermarkets examining sodium contents on the nutrition labels, and found one at Woolworths that is 124mg/100g. It's jumbo size, tail on, de-veined, cooked
- frozen mussels - 1 packet
- as above, I have found one 157mg/100g sodium. The bag I bought would provide several meals. *Alternative*: Some seafood mixtures - e.g. Seafood marinara - might contain pieces of fish as well. That's all good too!
- 5-6 fresh tomatoes, chopped
- 1 tin chopped tomatoes (optional)
- 1 large onion (doesn't matter which kind, but I like Spanish onions)
- 2 cloves garlic
- 6 or more button mushrooms
- *Kick Start* Hot Chilli Sauce - a good blob, depending how hot you like your food
- olive oil - about 2 tablespoons
- a splash of no-alcohol red wine (optional)
- parsley for garnish (optional)

100

Method

The spaghetti will probably take longer to cook than the sauce. I recommend putting the water on to boil before starting the sauce, and then add the spaghetti at boiling point.

1. Ahead of time, defrost the prawns and mussels. They have been cooked already, and if you add them to the mixture to thaw, they will get a bit tough.
2. Put the water on to boil for spaghetti in a large pot.
3. Wash and chop fresh tomatoes into cubes.
4. Chop onion into rough pieces. Crush garlic.
5. Wash and slice button mushrooms.
6. Heat olive oil in pan. When hot, add onion and cook until soft. Stir to avoid burning.
7. Add garlic. Don't add the garlic with the onion as it cooks more quickly and will burn. Stir for a minute or so.
8. Add chopped tomatoes.
9. Add dash of red wine and hot chilli sauce. If you haven't used it before, start with an amount the size of a five cent piece. After tasting, you can always add more if you want.
10. Keep an eye on it, stirring occasionally for about 5 minutes.
11. When tomatoes have softened, add the sliced button mushrooms. Allow to cook until softened. Cover the pot to avoid drying out.
12. If you prefer a juicier sauce, add the tin of chopped tomatoes now. Turn it down to low.
13. When your spaghetti is cooked and ready to drain, add the prawns and mussels and allow to heat through. Taste the sauce to make sure it is warm, and taste a mussel to see if heated through.
14. Taste again to decide whether you want any more hot chilli sauce. *Serve and enjoy!*

Cod and Lemon

serves: 2 **prep:** 10 minutes **cooking time:** 20 minutes

I watched my Aunty Gladys bake this for dinner (with sea perch) many times when I visited her in the hot and humid Mackay, visiting her on weekends to escape the mining town I was teaching at. The sea perch always tasted fresh with that citrus zing. Sometimes she would add slices of tomato on top as well. Salad on the side with a salad dressing. I use cod as sea perch can be higher in sodium ~ Julieann

Ingredients

- 1 fillet of cod or fish of your choice per foil wrap
- 1 lemon
- olive oil or dob of butter

Change it up: add
- pepper

- thyme
- rosemary

- garlic

- diced onion

- parsley
- chives

- Italian herbs

- dill
- basil
- tarragon

- tomato slices
- spinach
- sliced capsicum

Or your own herbs and spices or even veggies. You can also use salmon for this recipe.

Method

1. Heat oven to 200º C.
2. Cut lemon in half - use the juice of one half and slice up the other half.
3. Lay foil flat on a baking tray.
4. Place the fish in the centre of the alfoil.
5. Cover it with the lemon slices, and whatever you would like to add on top, according to your tastes.
6. Fold up the sides of the alfoil and fold the foil together in the middle, sealing the tops and sides well.
7. Bake in the oven for 15-20 minutes.

Serve with a garden salad on the side, and a dash of salad dressing.

Fish Tacos

serves: 6 **prep:** 15 minutes **cooking time:** 10 minutes

I was at school teaching, and had a spare lesson, but ended up covering for a teacher in food technology. The students had to cook fish tacos, so I had a very steep learning curve on how to cook this (pretending to know what I was doing). I watched the students enjoy devouring their creations afterwards while they reflected on the process and the flavours and how they would change it next time, if they needed to - Julieann

Ingredients

Fish
- white fish of your choice - I like cod or barramundi
- 1 lime
- olive oil
- ⅓ cup plain flour
- ½ teaspoon pepper
- Add ½ teaspoon of cayenne and ½ teaspoon cumin if you like

Filling
- Basically salad ingredients, all sliced and diced
- purple cabbage
- avocado
- tomatoes
- corn kernels
- red onion (I leave this out for my tacos)
- you can purchase a cabbage slaw if you like
- grated cheese if you are able to have cheese, or use mozzarella is low sodium, unsalted Gouda cheese, quark cheese

Dressing
- homemade mayo (p63) or sour cream, or store bought mayonnaise if you tolerate it
- white corn tortillas

Method

1. Prepare the filling first, dicing and chopping so you can assemble your fish taco with the fish is still warm.
2. Make the homemade mayo if you are using it.
3. Mix together plain flour and pepper and leave on a small plate. Add the cumin and cayenne here as well if you want.
4. Cut the fish into smaller pieces, then coat them in the seasoned flour mix.
5. Cook the fish pieces in olive oil on a moderately hot stove setting until golden brown. Add a drizzle of lime juice if you like.
6. Drain the fish pieces on paper towel.
7. Assemble your fish tacos including mayo or sour cream.
8. Serve.

Add a squeeze of lime juice over the top.

My Dinners

Mmm ... Dessert

Mmm … Dessert

Dessert. A sweetness that ends a meal.
Or if you're a rebel, it begins a meal! Some people enjoy it each night.
Some only for *special occasions* or *dinner parties*.
Some people with Ménière's *avoid dessert* due to sugar content
possibly setting off their symptoms.
Other Menierians are fine with sugar. Go *figure!*

In the following pages are just a *few dessert recipes* sent in to us.
And of course, there's millions of dessert recipes in books and online if
you are searching for something specific that suits your *dietary needs*.

For those intolerant of sugar, Stevia may be a suitable substitute for you.
It's a safe natural sweetener, not made from lab chemicals. But research it first.
For 1 cup of sugar, use 1 teaspoon of Stevia + ⅓ of apple sauce.

Being a grown-up is the best,
you don't need permission
to have dessert for dinner.

My dinner stomach is full,
but my dessert stomach still has room.

Cake is the answer, no matter the question.

Mmm ... Dessert

I love homemade apple pie!

Apples baked with dates and cinnamon in the centre and *since I was born in Canada*, pumpkin pie.

Fruit salad.

Chocolate self-saucing pudding.

Apple pie or crumble with sliced apple instead of diced. Panna cotta is amazing too!

I love Pavlova!

I like to put a spread of Greek yoghurt, sliced strawberries on top and a few chocolate chips on top of that on some baking paper and put it into the freezer. When it's frozen, break it into chunks.

Two homemade peanut butter chocolate chip cookies with ice-cream in the middle!

All sorts of fruit with a yoghurt dip.

I love my sugar-free strawberry cheesecake. No baking!

Did you say ... dessert?

Brownie Bliss Balls - *yum!*

I do a low-sugar banana bread. *I love to* freeze slices of it to take to work for morning tea.

Baked apples - core the apple and place walnuts and sultanas inside, sprinkle with cinnamon and pop into the microwave for up to 7 minutes. Sometimes *I serve it* with ice-cream or yoghurt.

Chocolate dipped strawberries.

Trifle hits the spot for me. Jam roll, sliced, jelly and custard. I check the sodium levels on these as well.

Apple crumble. Homemade. With custard or ice-cream.

Grilled bananas, crushed macadamias and yoghurt. *Sometimes I drizzle* caramel sauce over the top.

Lemon-blueberry scones with a bit of a sprinkle of sugar on top.

Crepes with fruit and yoghurt or chocolate sauce.

Cumquat (or Orange) and Almond Cake

serves: 8 **prep:** 40 minutes **cooking time:** 50 minutes

This recipe was donated by Ruth. This flourless cake is popular in the Sephardi world, with origins in the Iberian peninsula. Variations of this cake can be found from Spain, the Mediterranean, and even further east to Iran.

Ingredients

- 300g cumquats or 2 oranges
- 2½ cups almond meal (or self ground almonds) or optionally, replace ½ cup of almond meal with ½ cup sifted self-raising flour.
- 125g unsalted butter, softened
- 1 cup caster sugar
- 5 eggs
- 2 teaspoons of *Salt Skip* baking powder (I get it from lowsodiumfoods.com.au)

Syrup

- 2 tablespoons of cumquat or orange juice
- ½ cup caster sugar
- ½ cup water

Serving

If you like, you can dust it with icing sugar and serve with Greek yoghurt.

Method

Preparing cumquats:

1. Cover cumquats (skin and all) with water in a saucepan.
2. Bring to boil and then simmer for 10 minutes until soft, then cool. *If using oranges* they need about 20-30 minutes simmering.
3. Set aside when soft to cool.
4. Cut into pieces and remove the seeds.

(I sometimes get a huge batch of cumquats from a local tree. I freeze them into 300g lots to make future cakes, especially out of cumquat season)

Cooking

1. Preheat oven to 180º C (fan forced).
2. Use a 22cm cake tin - grease the sides and bottom, and line the bottom with baking paper.
3. Mix the cooked cumquats (including skins) and the other ingredients until smooth.
4. Put in the cake tin and bake for one hour or until a skewer comes out clean. I usually check from about 45 minutes baking.

Making the syrup:

1. Place the ingredients into a small saucepan and simmer 5 minutes.
2. Make holes all over the top of the cake with a metal skewer and spoon warm syrup over as soon as it comes out of the oven. The syrup will be absorbed into the cake.

Pumpkin Cheesecake

serves: 8 **prep:** 15 minutes **cooking time:** 1 hour 30 minutes

Cheesecake originated in ancient Greece over 2,000 years ago when it was simply a mixture of cheese, flour and honey. In the 19th century cream cheese was invented and then it evolved. This recipe came from Diana, who was born in Canada and makes this pumpkin pie for Canada Day every year.

Ingredients

- 500g cream cheese
- 325g *Mungalli* Organic Ricotta Cheese
- 800g pumpkin puree
- ¾ dark brown sugar
- ¾ cup raw sugar
- 4 large eggs
- 1 teaspoon ground cinnamon
- ¼ teaspoon ground cloves
- ¼ teaspoon ground nutmeg
- ¼ teaspoon ground ginger
- ¼ teaspoon ground mace
- 1½ tablespoons gluten free flour
- 2 teaspoons vanilla extract

Method

1. Beat 500g cream cheese until soft.
2. Add 325g *Mungalli* organic ricotta cheese
3. Add and mix:
   800g pumpkin puree
   ¾ dark brown sugar
   ¾ cup raw sugar
4. Add and mix:
   4 large eggs
   1 teaspoon ground cinnamon
   ¼ teaspoon ground cloves
   ¼ teaspoon ground nutmeg
   ¼ teaspoon ground ginger
   ¼ teaspoon ground mace
   1½ tablespoons gluten free flour
   2 teaspoons vanilla extract
5. Pour into greased ramekins, or into a pie crust - homemade or pre-made.
6. Bake at 170º C for 30 minutes.
7. Reduce to 150º C for 45 minutes to 1 hour depending on if you have small ramekins or a whole pie.

Serve with a dollop of cream (optional).

Gluten Free Lemon Polenta Cake

serves: 8 **prep:** 20 minutes **cooking time:** 20 minutes

This delicious cake was sent to us by Ruth. Polenta is finely ground cornmeal. It's a northern Italian staple and acts as a gluten-free alternative for flour in baking. During the WWII years, it was eaten out of necessity. It's low in fat and a good source of complex carbohydrates, fibre and antioxidants. This lemon polenta cake is super delicious!

Ingredients

- 220g softened unsalted butter
- 90g caster sugar
- 3 eggs at room temperature
- 210g almond meal
- 115g Polenta
- 1 teaspoon *Salt Skip* baking powder
- finely grated zest 2 large lemons
- juice of 1½ large lemons
- A handful of currants (about ½ cup)

Method

1. Soak the currants in lemon juice while collecting ingredients.
2. Preheat oven to 160º C (fan-forced).
3. Line a 30 x 21cm slice tray with baking paper to come up the sides.
4. Cream butter and sugar, then add eggs one at a time.
5. Gently fold in almonds, polenta, baking powder zest, juice and currants.
6. Bake about 20 minutes until golden and just cooked.
7. Remove from oven and cover with a plate to finish cooking, retain heat and moisture.

For a citrus topping, combine 2 tablespoons of granulated sugar with the juice of one lemon. Don't leave the sugar to dissolve. Then spread the syrup over the cake.

This cake can also be served with lemon curd if desired.

** The photograph shows lemon polenta cake without currants, and drizzled with vanilla icing.

Spring Fruit Panna Cotta

serves: 5 **prep:** 20 minutes **cooking time:** 5-6 *hours*

Wendy gave us this lovely fresh dessert. Panna Cotta is a classic Italian custard and is a frequently requested dessert. It originated in Piedmont, Italy, home to Fiat, Nutella and Lavazza Coffee. Wendy has the beautiful additions of gold kiwi fruit, passionfruit, chopped crystal ginger and green grapes on top that makes a feast for our eyes as well as our stomachs.

Ingredients

- 100mL *Tamar Valley* Greek style yoghurt
- 300mL thickened cream
- ⅓ cup honey
- 80mL lime juice
- grated zest of 1 lime
- 1¼ teaspoons of gelatine powder

Topping:

- 2 gold kiwi fruit cut into smallish pieces
- About 8-10 green grapes cut into 3 or 4 pieces
- 3 passionfruit pulp
- 1 tablespoon finely chopped crystal ginger
- 1 tablespoon caster sugar
- 1 tablespoon lime juice extra
- mint sprig

Or fruits of your choice.

Method

1. Stir cream, honey, lime zest and juice over low heat until honey melts and the mixture is heated through.
2. Add the yoghurt and set aside.
3. Sprinkle the gelatine powder on a tablespoon or so of warm water, or lime juice, and allow to dissolve then mix into the cream mixture.
4. Lightly oil 5 x ½ cup moulds or muffin holes, divide cream mixture evenly.

Refrigerate for 5-6 hours or overnight.

1. About 1 hour prior to serving, mix all topping ingredients. Set aside.
2. Gently invert panna cotta from moulds, spoon fruit and juices over and add a mint sprig.

Apple Pie

serves: 8 **prep:** 30 minutes **cooking time:** 40 minutes

Apple pie is contentious in my household. One of my three kids hates cooked fruit (so she misses out on this delish dessert - she eats the custard and ice-cream that accompanies the apple pie). The baby of the family (26 years old at the time of print of this cookbook) loves apple pie and sometimes requests it for his birthday cake ~ Julieann

Ingredients

Pastry
- 350g plain flour
- 225g no-salt butter
- 50g caster sugar
- 2 eggs

Apple Filling
- 6 cups sliced green apples (or apples of your choice)
- 350mL unsweetened apple juice
- 3 tablespoons cornstarch
- 1 tablespoon ground cinnamon

Sprinkle of caster sugar for the top if you like. *These are also good as mini apple pies.*

Method

Pastry
1. Mix butter and sugar in a bowl until just mixed.
2. Add 1 egg, and the yolk of the other (keep the egg white for later).
3. Beat it until it looks scrambled.
4. Use a wooden spoon and add flour slowly (it will clump into a ball). Use hands to finish the mixing.
5. Cover with cling wrap and put it in the fridge for 45 minutes.
6. Roll out the pastry to fit a pie dish, leaving enough for the top of the pie.

Filling
1. Whisk the cornstarch, ⅓ apple juice and cinnamon and put aside.
2. With remaining apple juice, simmer the apple slices until tender.
3. Stir in cornstarch/apple juice/cinnamon mix and simmer until thickened.
4. Spoon mixture into pastry pie dish, cover with the crust. Seal the edges and put in some cuts for steam vents. Brush with left over egg white (or weave the top pastry to be fancy).
5. Bake at 180° C for around 40-45 minutes until it is golden brown on top. Add a sprinkle of sugar on the top if you like.

Serve with custard or ice-cream if you like.

Quark Cheesecake

serves: 6-8 **prep:** 15 minutes **cooking time:** 1 hour

Quark (quarg) is a dairy product, and is a soft, white and unaged cheese with no-salt added. I've found this recipe difficult to find, but makes a great cheesecake. It satisfies that desire to have cheesecake. This recipe is adapted from a few recipes I found on the net ~ Francoise

Ingredients

- 175g castor sugar
- 100mL light oil, e.g. canola, sunflower, etc
- 5 eggs
- 900g Quark Cheese
- 2 teaspoons vanilla essence/extract
- 2 teaspoons lemon juice
- 120g flour
- 2 teaspoons *Salt Skip* baking powder

Optional: Enough almond meal to cover 5mm on the bottom of the tin.
Optional: Rum soaked raisins - 1 cup raisins to ¼ cup rum overnight or a chopped apple or place slices on the bottom of the pan.

The cheesecake will shrink a bit when it cools down and mine did not slump in the middle as some recipes suggested it might happen. Other recipes had crusts but I considered it a fiddle and did not have time to make it, hence the almond meal and it worked fine. I used the raisins, but will rum soak them next time.

Method

1. Preheat oven to 175º C, lower if fan forced.
2. Prepare a spring form round tin by first greasing it lightly and then using 2 layers of baking paper.
3. You will need to cut out the rounds for the bottom. Then use strips to line around the sides of the tin.
4. If you are using the almond meal, evenly spread it into the tin by shaking it evenly about. It makes a nice soft crust at the bottom of the cake as well as adding a little flavour.
5. Beat the eggs and vanilla essence (can use an egg beater, I did).
6. Add in oil and sugar and beat until well combined.
7. Add in the Quark Cheese and mix well.
8. Add in the lemon juice and mix well.
9. Fold in the sifted flour and baking powder and mix well, but don't over beat it.
10. Fold in the raisins/apples if using.
11. Pour mixture gently into the baking tin.
12. Bake for 1 hour, or until a skewer comes out clean.

Let it cool and enjoy.
Can serve with strawberries or blueberries or both.

My Desserts

Party Food

When you have a function, aren't you're invited to a party
there's a lot much to consider:

the food, the noise, any visual stimulus, the music...

Then there's 'how do I *feel* today?
Will I have a vertigo attack while I'm out and about,
what's my rescue plan?

In the next few pages you'll find suggested safe low-salt foods
to take with you to parties, if you need to take a plate to share.
If in doubt about a party, be sure to eat at home before you go.

A party without cake
is really just a meeting.

Party food is
always worth fighting for!

A child having a tea party with a teddy bear
"Would you like anything to eat Mr. Bear?"
"No thanks, I'm stuffed."

Party Food

I tread very carefully just have small amounts and drink plenty of water.

Potato bake is my go to dish to take. Easy to make without any salt and still yummy for everyone. Also salad with low-sodium dressings. I will often take my own protein. If it's a BBQ I will bring a piece of steak and make sure it doesn't get seasoned. Most of my family and friends try to accommodate me to some degree. I will often say don't worry and that I will bring something for myself (I don't like making it hard for anyone).

I'll take a plate of nibbles, no cheese cause I'm dairy free too! But lots of veggies, low-sodium crackers or plain corn chips.

I will often take cut up veggies with either a homemade or low salt dip with unsalted nuts and fruit and a cheese and quince paste to make it a bit fancy for a party. For a salad, I will make any kind of salad but with a homemade dressing, ie potato salad, homemade mayo etc. I went to a 70's themed party a few months ago and took devilled eggs. It's true I didn't stay for all the dancing but it was great fun while it lasted! I also do the 'eat something' before I go out so I'm not overly hungry, particularly if it's someone I don't know well, and I don't want to have to give the whole explanation! And I watch my sodium intake that day so I can afford a bit of extra unintended sodium.

Celery and carrot and homemade salt-free hummus and tzatziki.

I've always had to wait until the day of the party before saying whether I can even attend or not. Then if I've been good I eat minimum food or choose wisely.

I make homemade sausage rolls. Use any sausage roll recipe you like, *omitting salt*. There are recipes on the Internet for beef, chicken or non-meat 'sausage' rolls, using for example sweet potato and kidney beans or chickpeas. *I always make sure to* spice it up a bit in flavour using some Kick Start Hot Chilli Sauce (if not obtainable locally, you can buy at *lowsodiumfoods.com.au*) - this is my go-to flavour enhancer. You don't need much, just about half a teaspoon, but if you like things a bit hotter, add some more! Use Pampas Butter Puff Pastry. It has 110mg/100g of sodium ~ Sally

I like to risk turkey-cranberry roll-ups, sometimes when I'm feeling really brave, I add some bacon bits. Spread 3 tortillas with 250g cream cheese between them. Add ¼ cup dried cranberries, a green onion thinly sliced, and a slice of turkey (add bacon if you're brave). Roll them tightly before wrapping in plastic wrap and chill. Slice them before serving.

Party Food

I take a fruit platter with red and green grapes on sticks, kiwi fruit, mango, strawberries, blueberries, raspberries, pineapple, banana, rockmelon, and watermelon and add a Greek yoghurt for dipping.

Because I love apple in my salad, I make a low-sodium Waldorf Salad. It always goes down well at parties.

I wouldn't normally attend because the hyperacusis, aural fullness and hearing loss make it too hard to socialise. *If* I went, I would eat the fruit, if that was on offer. I might have a very small amount of cheese because, cheese! Otherwise *I tend to eat before I go*, so I'm not really hungry and can go without eating if I need to. If I was to take a share plate it would be vegetables with a homemade dip (e.g. hummus or tzatziki) or fruit.

I like to make a dish of low-sodium Mexican Layered Dip, using a homemade refried beans recipe, then adding layers of low-sodium refried beans, sour cream, mashed avocado (with a little lime juice), shredded lettuce and chopped tomatoes. I put a bowl of low-sodium corn chips next to it for dipping.

I mix together 3 - 4 mashed avocado, 2 medium tomatoes chopped, ¼ red onion and juice of 1 lime as an avocado dip. Use veggie sticks or crackers for dipping.

I take low-sodium Buffalo Chicken Dip, with a plate of raw veggies - carrot sticks, celery sticks, zucchini sticks, cucumber sticks, low-sodium crackers, etc

I make up a no-salt macaroni salad.

Mango Spring rolls. You know, the ones wrapped in rice paper. Inside I add vermicelli noodles, carrots, cucumber, sometimes mango, lettuce. Sometimes I add shredded chicken. *I do a* low-sodium dipping sauce to go with it.

Sometimes at parties I watch normal people eat anything without a care. I blink, and take a bite out of my carrot stick/celery peanut butter duo.

If I'm feeling really crappy, I take a plate of fresh, crisp, rolled up lettuce and watch facial expressions of people after they take their first bite.

Avocado devilled eggs, leaving out the ¼ teaspoon of salt. *Yum!*

Watermelon cups - cubed watermelon with finely chopped cucumber, red onion, chopped fresh mint and lime juice sprinkled on top. *It's a party for your tastebuds!*

Dizzy Fairy Bread

serves: 12 **prep:** 10 minutes **cooking time:** 0

This is an Aussie classic. We all grew up going to parties where fairy bread was on the table, and it was devoured instantly. They're in my #1 Amazon bestseller novel with a main MD character - 'The Colour of Broken' (Amelia Grace), when the characters are raising money to donate to Ménière's research. Vertigo Meringues as well ~ Julieann

Ingredients

- soft white low-sodium bread (or homemade)
- low-salt or unsalted butter
- 100s and 1000s sprinkles (the round ones)

Method

1. Grab a slice of fresh bread.
2. Use a knife to add a spread of butter.
3. Cut the slice into 2 triangles, or 4.
4. Shake 100s and 1000s on top.
5. On repeat for as many slices of bread that you want to use.
6. Eat.

Vertigo Meringues

serves: 20 **prep:** 10 minutes **cooking time:** 1 hour 30 minutes

Ingredients

- 3 eggs whites
- 175g caster sugar
- pinch of cream of tartar
- ½ teaspoon vanilla essence

Method

1. Preheat oven to 120º C.
2. Add egg whites to a large bowl and whisk with an electric mixer until soft peaks form.
3. Add pinch of cream of tartar, then caster sugar, one tablespoon at a time, ensuring it is dissolved after each tablespoonful. I usually rub a small amount of the mixture between my fingers to check that it is dissolved.
4. Add vanilla essence and whisk.
5. Put the meringue mixture into a piping bag, then pipe meringue swirls onto baking paper on an oven tray.
6. Pop them into the oven, then reduce heat to 90º C, and bake for 1 hour 30 minutes, leaving them to cool in the oven.
7. They can be stored in an airtight container for up to a week (if they last that long).

Vanilla Swirl Cupcakes aka Vertigo Cupcakes

serves: 22 mini cupcakes **prep**: 10 minutes **cooking time**: 9-11 minutes

I remember when I was young, helping Mum make cupcakes. I'd lick the beaters of course. This recipe, from memory, is a favourite with my kids and others who come to our table. They're kind of moorish, but when they're mini cupcakes, that's a good thing. I also make them for my dog's birthday each year, leaving out the vanilla essence. They're in my #1 Amazon novel with a main MD character - 'The Colour of Broken' ~ Amelia Grace

Ingredients

Cupcake mix

- 3 tablespoons of salt-reduced butter
- ⅓ cup of caster sugar
- 1 egg
- teaspoon of vanilla essence
- 1 cup self-raising flour
- 50mL milk

Icing

- 1½ cups of soft icing sugar
- 1 tablespoon of salt-reduced butter
- 1 tablespoon of milk or water

Add some food colouring if you like, or hundreds and thousands, or store bought icing cake decorations like flowers or dinosaurs etc.

Method

Cupcake mix

1. Heat the oven to 160°C.
2. Add the butter and caster sugar to a mixing bowl and mix until the butter is light and creamy.
3. Add the egg and mix well.
4. Add the vanilla essence and mix.
5. Add half of the self-raising flour and mix till combined.
6. Add half of the milk and mix.
7. Add the remaining flour and mix, then the remaining milk.
8. The mixture should be a smooth, soft consistency, like thick porridge.
9. Add large teaspoons to the cake paper in the cupcake pan, and place into the oven. I usually put the timer on the oven for 9 minutes. They are baked when the cake springs back when touched. If they're not ready, bake them for 2-3 minutes more.

Icing

Combine icing sugar, butter and milk/water in a mixing bowl and mix with a wooden spoon until it is smooth but not too runny. I usually cut off the corner of a snap lock bag and spoon the icing into it, then pipe it onto the cupcakes in a spinning swirl shape - Vertigo Cupcakes. *Decorate like an artist!*

My Party Foods

BBQ

BBQ

The *great outdoors* and BBQs.
Our summertime relaxation with family and friends.
Think grilled meats, burgers, sausages, ribs, seafood, corn on the cob, salads, potato salad, coleslaw and breads and buns. Potato bake!

And immediately we know you think, *'How high is the salt content?'*

We've just included low-sodium *meat rubs* and *condiments* here, not actual BBQ recipes, to help make your meat and salads a little more *flavoursome*.

There's no problem that a BBQ can't solve.

Sorry, I can't hear you over
the sizzle of the BBQ and my tinnitus.

BBQ: The only time it's acceptable to play with your food.

BBQ Rubs & Marinades

Chicken Seasonings and Rubs (p12-13)

chicken spice rub, Italian chicken seasoning mix, smoky spicy - a little sweet, chicken all purpose seasoning, smoked paprika chicken rub, Greek seasoning mix, spice chicken rub, chicken seasoning with ground mustard, french onion blend, cajun blend

Beef, Pork & Lamb Seasonings and Rubs (p14-15)

Cajun blend, chilli seasoning, Italian seasoning blend, Mediterranean blend, ranch salad blend, seasoned blend, spice blend recipe, taco seasoning, beefy blend with mustard, curry powder alternative, flavoursome steak & veggie seasoning, steakhouse spice rub, BBQ steak rub, pork rub, lamb rub, lamb dry spice rub, pork beer crispy crackling (p94)

Seafood Seasonings (p16)

fish blend, lemon & garlic, herbs, Cajun fish seasoning, crab, prawn, oyster seasoning

BBQ Rubs & Marinades

On my chicken - equal parts smoked paprika, chilli powder, garlic powder, onion powder, cumin, brown sugar, course ground black pepper, ½ measure of mustard powder, ¼ measure cinnamon.

I always keep a spice jar of 1 part course black pepper, ½ part granulated garlic and onion. I add other ingredients depending on what I feel like. For example, I grab a tablespoon and add some thyme and rosemary, or chilli powder, or other spices. It alters the flavor and is an easy way to alter flavor to your taste.

Salt-free BBQ rubs can be made by combining sweet and smoky spices like smoked paprika and brown sugar with savory elements such as garlic powder, onion powder, and chilli powder. You can also add other spices like cumin, black pepper, and cayenne for depth and heat.

I mix together brown sugar, paprika, pepper, garlic powder and use it as a rub.

I like to use Herbie's ZALT - It's Not Salt. It adds a bright tangy flavour.

BBQ Rubs & Marinades

I love a good rump beef on the BBQ. The rub I like to use is a bit sweet and spicy. I just grab the shakers and sprinkle these over the meat - onion powder, black pepper, a little of cayenne (not too much), some brown sugar, garlic powder and paprika. I rub it over the meat and leave it sit for a few minutes before BBQing.

I leave the BBQ to my husband, and because he's journeyed with me for more than 30 years with my Ménière's, he knows my sodium limits. One that he does that I particularly like on lamb (for Australia Day) is a marinade (he leaves is on for about 4 hours), and has cumin, lemon juice, Greek yoghurt, and a pinch of cayenne. He said it's supposed to have coriander as well, but I'm one of those people who is in the 'I hate coriander!' club, so he leaves it out and substitutes it with cumin instead.

I really miss BBQ sauce but have played around with this rub for pork, chicken, ribs and even salmon. It's similar to BBQ sauce, I think. Play around with the measurements to what suits your tastebuds - ½ cup ground mustard (or paprika), ½ cup brown sugar, for on pork, but can leave out for chicken), 1 tablespoon chilli powder, 1 tablespoon ground black pepper, 1 tablespoon garlic powder, 1 tablespoon onion powder, 1 teaspoon dried thyme or cayenne pepper (optional).

This is my favourite salt-free BBQ rub - 1 teaspoon onion powder, 1 teaspoon cumin, 1 tablespoon brown sugar, ⅛ teaspoon allspice, 1 teaspoon granulated garlic, 1 teaspoon smoked paprika, 1 teaspoon chilli powder, ¼ teaspoon dry mustard. For more heat add cayenne pepper or chilli flakes to taste. Change it up, add black pepper, oregano, cumin, mustard powder or thyme. *If you like it sweet,* use brown sugar. I've noted that some recipes add finely ground coffee for an earthy flavour.

Low Sodium Foods Australia (Online) Pouches of Flavour Bombs

- pork rub, meatball & mince, spicy chicken, BBQ steak rub, salmon rub, Moroccan spice seasoning, king creole (Cajun seasoning), ras el hanout (North African seasoning), chemoula (Moroccan Seasoning), shawarma (Turkish Seasoning), berbere (Ethiopian Seasoning), Sumac (Moroccan Spice)

Check out these online low-sodium spices for BBQs:
- SmokeyQ
- Spice Zen
- Spice Road Spices
- Herbie's Spices
- Etsy
- Dash (completely no-salt based in Canada)
- Memphis Dust
- Meathead

Salad Dressings

Dijon mustard (0mg sodium per 10g)... the *Hill Farm* one. *I use it in* salad dressing or part of a marinade for meat. *It has lot of flavour* so you don't notice the lack of salt.

I like to do Teriyaki Sauce with reduced sodium, honey, garlic and fresh chopped ginger. The recipe is on p16.

Honey Mustard Sauce *for me and my family* when we do fish on the BBQ. It's got whole grain mustard, honey, garlic and red pepper flakes.

Lemon and herb - honey, olive oil, lemon juice, basil and dijon mustard.

I like this sweeter salad dressing on my green leaf goodness so the cows don't come and eat it off my plate (I'm not a fan of plain salads. I find then unbelievably boring - it's the dressing that gives the salad a signature) - ¼ cup maple syrup, ½ teaspoon ground ginger, ¼ cup apple cider vinegar, ½ teaspoon ground black pepper, 1 teaspoon of sesame oil, 1 minced garlic clove, 2 teaspoons of reduced sodium soy sauce. Shake it up. Keeps the cows away from my salads for up to a week.

Low Sodium Foods, Australia (Online)

- *Attitude Dressing*: the ultimate salad dressing or sauce - canola & olive oil, vinegar, water, egg yolk, mustard, garlic, herbs and spices, salt and pepper. Try it also with fish or chicken, or poured over steamed rice or baked potatoes.

- Maleny Cuisine Italian Style Salad Dressing - combines vinegar, with garlic, sugar and a blend of Italian herbs and spices. Splash over your favourite vegetable or fruit salad.

- Maleny Cuisine Sweet Mustard Salad Dressing - combines vinegar, with garlic, sugar and mustard seeds together with a blend of other herbs and spices. Add to your favourite vegetable or fruit salad. It's great splashed over a green salad with nuts.

- Maleny Cuisine Thai Style Salad Dressing - combines vinegar, with garlic, chilli, lemongrass, sugar and a blend of other herbs and spices. Splash over your favourite salad or combine with poached chicken, avocado and mango for something different.

- Red Kellys Basil & Garlic Dressing

- Red Kellys Lemon Myrtle Dressing

- Red Kellys Sweet Chilli & Lime Dressing

- Red Kellys Tangy Traditional Dressing

Search for Low-Sodium Salad Dressings on the Internet. Great flavours.

My BBQ Recipes

Christmas

Imagine sitting at a Christmas table with just *Menierians*...
We wouldn't have to worry about *too much salt* because the food would be prepared to *perfection*. We wouldn't have to worry about too much *noise* because we would all be *considerate* of each other. And we wouldn't get annoyed with anyone if they didn't *hear* properly.

Back to reality. Christmas is a time of family, friends and the *festive spirit*, however you celebrate, but people with Ménière's have so much *more to consider* before even taking a seat at the *Christmas table*. Our constant thoughts are, 'How much sodium is in that food?'

We hope, the next pages help you *navigate* Christmas day, and with the *Christmas menus* we have planned for you, takes the stress out of wondering *what to serve*. Enjoy your Christmas *crackers* and hats and jokes, and that *cricket game* and swimming if you are able, or snow angels, or snow people, or just sitting by a fireplace.

Merry Christmas!

Christmas calories don't count, right?

Do Santa's cookies pair well with wine?
Asking for a friend.

Just be your-elf.

Christmas

I have Ménière's and type 2 diabetes which is managed by a low carb diet. I go to my daughters for lunch and dinner and because she lives close to my house. I pre-cook both meals and heat them in the microwave at her house. Lunch is a chicken thigh fillet cooked in my air fryer with 300g of the chats and I grate 40g of Norco natural cheese on top of the chats. Dinner is a chicken thigh fillet, 250g of the chats and two large mushrooms I peel and remove the stems and put 35g of Norco cheese on them before I cook them in the oven for 20 minutes. *I refuse to eat anything different to what I normally do so I don't get sick.* I have a varied diet but cook these meals for Christmas Day because they both microwave easily.

We always do cold meats and salad - I usually hunt for a lightly smoked ham (usually a butcher and then cold chicken or turkey and seafood - with homemade salads - dessert is usually pavlova and banoffee pie.

I like to eat roasted turkey and roast potatoes, carrots and brussel sprouts. Plus *I like to drink* bubbly Devondale Sparkler Grape juice.

Unsalted nuts are always a go to when they are sitting on the table. *My dad likes to* buy the shelled nuts and cracks them himself, then shares them with me.

We cook roast lamb and the vegetables without the salt. Always have. Always will. There are salt shakers on the table if anyone wants to add their own salt.

When I am suss about how much salt is on the roast meat, I just dig into the roast veggies instead, which I LOVE.

I always volunteer to take a dish or a plate of food. That way, I know it is safe for me to eat. I always let them know that if I don't eat something, it's because of my Ménière's and low salt that I have to follow.

Christmas

I find that fish, chicken and turkey are good low-sodium choices for me for Christmas if they are prepared from scratch.

Last year I stumbled upon a really funky salad that I love. It's got spinach leaves, strawberries, walnuts, rocket leaves, mint leaves, salt-reduced feta cheese (sometimes I don't eat the feta) and a drizzle of balsamic vinegar. It looks Christmassy with the red and green.

I do a tall jug of iced water and throw all sorts fruits into it. It always looks great on the table, and is a thirst quencher.

I always take my own homemade Christmas food to family gatherings. Many of them have seen me have a vertigo attack, and so they understand perfectly the effects of me consuming too much salt.

I'm careful with my food choices, but I am exhausted for a couple of days later, with all the noise and the chatter and the loud laughing and tracking who is speaking to try and hear what they are saying.

We incorporate a dish of salmon into the family menu for me. I add the no-salt vegetables and green vegetables from the roasts.

I have the same plate of food as everyone else at the Christmas table, but only take little bites of food that I suspect has a high sodium content. If salt and pepper shakers are on the table, I know that the food has been cooked without salt, which I am totally thankful for.

Christmas Day Cold Menu

Nibbles

Egg Nog
Mince Pies
Rumbles
Reindeer Droppings
Gingerbread

Main Course

Cold Meats
lamb beef ham turkey chicken
Seafood
salmon prawns crab lobster mussels oysters
Salads & other Dishes

Dessert

Fig & Cherry Cake
Julieann's Pavlova
Royal Family Christmas Pudding
Individual Rhubarb and Apple Crumble
Christmas Gingernut Ripple Cake
Christmas Fruit Salad Tree
Nan's Traditional Custard

Christmas Day Roast Menu

Nibbles

Egg Nog
Mince Pies
Rumbles
Reindeer Droppings
Gingerbread

Main Course

Roast Lamb
Roast Beef
Roast Pork
Roast Chicken
Roast Turkey
Ham
Roast Vegetables

Dessert

Fig & Cherry Cake
Julieann's Pavlova
Royal Family Christmas Pudding
Individual Rhubarb and Apple Crumble
Christmas Gingernut Ripple Cake
Christmas Fruit Salad Tree
Nan's Traditional Custard

Rumbles (mis-heard Rumballs - thanks Ménière's)

makes: 30 **prep:** 10 minutes **cooking time:** 0 minutes

I love the season of Christmas. My daughter and I start placing Christmas decorations around the house in November to see if her dad notices (usually not). Claire and I also love to bake to Bing Crosby Christmas music. Here's our recipes for 'Rumbles' due to not hearing properly, Reindeer Droppings, and Claire's Gingerbread, our regular Christmas munchies that we have to top-up before for Christmas - Julieann

Ingredients

- 1 tin of condensed milk
- 8 Weet-Bix (if no rum - 9 if you add rum)
- ½ cup cocoa
- sultanas if you have to
- 2 tablespoons rum (optional)
- desiccated coconut for coating

Method

1. In a mixing bowl, crush up the Weet-Bix, then add the other ingredients except for the coconut. Mix in the rum is using.
2. Make into small balls and coat in coconut.
3. Refrigerate in an airtight container.

Enjoy!

Reindeer Droppings (how uncouth - Chocolate Truffles)

makes: 20 **prep:** 45 minutes **cooking time:** 0 minutes

These chocolate truffles are really delicious. We keep them in the fridge and eat them whenever, making up a new batch when we run out. For Christmas day, we make sure we have around 20 left, and I walk around to family, asking if they would like 'a reindeer dropping', with a straight face. I love the look they give me - Julieann

Ingredients

- 250g Arnott's Marie biscuits, crushed
- 1 can of condensed milk
- ⅓ cup cocoa
- ¼ desiccated coconut
- chocolate sprinkles for coating

Method

1. Crush the biscuits until they are fine dust and add to a bowl.
2. Add cocoa and coconut and mix.
3. Make a well in the centre and add the condensed milk, and, using a wooden spoon mix well.
4. Put in into the fridge for 30 minutes.
5. Pour chocolate sprinkles onto a plate, and roll tablespoons of mixture into balls, then roll in the chocolate sprinkles.
6. Refrigerate in an airtight container.

Enjoy!

Mince Pies

makes: 12 **prep:** 35 minutes **cooking time:** 25 minutes

Kim loves mince pies at Christmas. She makes them every year for her family. They have a family challenge - her son, who lives in Melbourne, always tries to find her low-sodium mince pies so she doesn't feel left out. He scours supermarkets & bakeries just for her to feel included. Then they have a mince pie taste off to see who's are better - haha - yep Kim's usually win. This of course is accompanied by a delicious glass of eggnog!

Ingredients

- 375g plain flour
- 250g unsalted butter
- 75g caster sugar, plus extra for sprinkling
- 1 egg
- 2 jars of bought 'fruit mince' (or make your own)

Method

1. In food processor (you can also do this by hand) add flour, sugar & butter and pulse for 5 seconds.
2. Add egg and mix until combined.
3. Tip out onto bench and form into a ball.
4. Shape into rectangle.
5. Wrap in glad wrap and pop in fridge for 15-20 minutes to cool.
6. Roll out pasty to about 3mm in thickness, cut out discs to fit your patty pan tray.
7. Spoon fruit mince into each base till ¾ full.
8. Cut 2 strips of pastry for a cross on top, or cut out another disc (slightly bigger) if you'd like a lid, or cut out star shapes.
9. Brush pastry with water to stick lid on.
10. Brush with egg wash and sprinkle with sugar.
11. Bake 160º C, 25 minutes.

Claire's Gingerbread

My daughter, Claire, makes this every year for end of year parties and for Christmas. She always comes home with an empty plate. It makes around 20, prep time 50 minutes, baking time 10 minutes.

125g butter, room temperature
½ cup golden syrup
½ cup brown sugar firmly packed
1 egg yolk
2½ cups plain flour
1 teaspoon mixed spice
1 tablespoon ground ginger
1 teaspoon bicarbonate soda

Icing
1 egg white, 1 cup pure icing sugar

- Preheat oven to 180º C and cover baking trays with baking paper, and lightly dust with flour.
- Beat butter and sugar until light and creamy.
- Add golden syrup and egg yolk and beat.
- Stir in flour and spices and bicarb soda and pop onto a floured surface and knead until smooth.
- Cover with plastic wrap and refrigerate 30 minutes.
- Roll our the dough to ½ cm thick and cut out shapes. Bake in over for 10 minutes or until brown. Cool.

Icing - Beat egg white until peaks form and then slowly add icing sugar. Pipe onto the gingerbread. Add colour to icing if you like.

Slow Cooked Roast Lamb & Veggies

serves: 6 **prep:** 40 minutes **cooking time:** 8 hours

When all the kids (they're all grownups but never act like it on Christmas Day) come home there's lots of laughter, too many Dad jokes from Paul, side-splitting wisecracks at each other, too much food, chocolate, & iced coffee all day (decaf for me), a glass of wine and usually a Nana nap. Oh and lots of tidbits for doggos Monty & Bear. Dinner is leftovers or cold meats & salad and some beers sitting around the fire pit outside under the stars ~ Kim.

Ingredients

- 2kg leg of lamb
- garlic olive oil
- fresh or dried rosemary

Gravy

- 25g unsalted butter
- 2-3 tablespoons plain flour
- juices from cook roast meat
- 2 teaspoons onion powder
- 1 teaspoon garlic powder
- 2 teaspoons mixed herbs, or your fav herbs
- 2 tablespoons *Quincy Jones* Jelly Worcestershire sauce (Low Sodium Foods Australia)
- 1 cup *Salt Skip* chicken or beef stock

Veggies Roasted in Duck Fat (or other oil)

- Potato
- Pumpkin
- Parsnip
- Carrot

1. Cut veggies into quarters, slightly larger than bite size.
2. Spray roasting pan with oil and place vegetables in, dollop duck fat around and bake for 1 hour at 180° C.

Serve with roast meat and gravy.

Method

1. Pour some garlic olive oil over the lamb and sprinkle with fresh or dried rosemary.
2. Roll up 4 pieces of foil and put them in the base of the slow cooker.
3. Place lamb on top.
4. Cook on low for 8 hours on low.
5. Use pan juices to make homemade gravy.

Tender, melts in your mouth and falls off the bone. Perfect.

Homemade Gravy

- Melt 25g unsalted butter in saucepan.
- Slowly whisk in 2-3 tablespoons of plain flour and whisk for 1 minute until smooth to cook out the flour.
- Pour juices from cooked roast meat into saucepan, whisking continuously.
- Add 2 teaspoons of onion powder.
- Add 1 teaspoon of garlic powder.
- Add 2 teaspoons of mixed herbs, or your favourite herbs.
- Add 2 tablespoons of QJJ Worcestershire sauce.
- Add 1 cup of *Salt Skip* chicken or beef stock – add more if needed, depends on amount of meat juices.

Whisk until thickened to your liking, serve.

Roast Lamb, Beef & Vegetables

serves: 6 **prep:** 20 minutes **cooking time:** lamb 2 hours beef - veggies 1 hour

My mum always cooked a roast lamb and vegetables for Christmas Day. She'd call it a 'Tom Cruise', and it was always delicious. She cooked it all in an electric fry pan using dripping (saved fats from previous roasts). Dad would cut up the meat while I tasted it. Now though, the Christmas lunch tradition is left with my family. I love to cook my roasts in olive oil - Julieann

Ingredients

Roast Lamb
2kg leg of lamb (2 hours 180º C)

Lamb Seasonings

- rosemary sprigs, 1 clove garlic
Cut garlic clove into slithers.
Pierce lamb with knife (at least 5 places) and insert garlic slithers, then rosemary sprigs.
(add a tablespoon of olive oil and a tablespoon of dijon mustard and brush over as well, if you like)

- 1 tablespoon olive oil, 4 cloves minced garlic, 1 tablespoon dijon mustard, 1½ teaspoons rosemary, 1½ teaspoons thyme, 2 teaspoons pepper

Combine all in a bowl and brush over the lamb before roasting. You can also score the top of the lamb before applying the rub.

Method

Roast Beef
1.3kg topside roast (1 hour 20 min 180º C)

Beef Seasonings

- 2 tablespoons black pepper, 2 tablespoons garlic powder, 1 tablespoon smoked paprika, 1 tablespoon onion powder, 1 teaspoon dried thyme, 1 teaspoon dried rosemary, 1 teaspoon ground cumin, 1 tablespoon of brown sugar (optional)

Combine all in a bowl and brush over the beef before roasting.

Mustard rub
- 2 tablespoons olive oil, 2 tablespoons dijon mustard, 2 teaspoons minced garlic, 2 teaspoons balsamic vinegar

Combine all in a bowl and brush over the lamb before roasting.

Roast Vegetables

1 hour before the roast is due to come out of the oven, throw in some vegetables into the same roasting pan. We usually have cut potatoes, pumpkin, sweet potato, whole small onions, carrots (sometimes we cut the carrot into sticks, steam them and then cook them in water with honey), brussel sprouts (I know, right?), cauliflower, broccoli, garlic cloves and whatever other vegetables you like to roast. You can sprinkle thyme and sage over the vegetables for extra flavour. My husband sometimes adds Italian Herbs (parsley, basil, oregano, thyme, marjoram and rosemary) to the veggies. Every twenty minutes turn the vegetables and brush them with the juices from the pan.

Roast Chicken & Turkey

serves: 6 **prep:** 10 minutes **cooking time:** chicken 2 hours, turkey mince roll 20 minutes

Kim gave us this wonderful roast chicken recipe. It's one they use at Christmas in the Mallee, a region in the north-west of Victoria. I love that she included the stuffing as well.

My family loves roast turkey, and my kids asked to celebrate thanksgiving in Australia just so they could have it. While store bought turkey is high in salt, I make this concoction with turkey mince - low salt - Julieann

Roast Chicken

- 1.8kg plain whole chicken

Gently rub sesame oil onto skin of chicken

Stuffing
1. Cut one whole lemon in half and stuff into cavity or make your own stuffing with: low-sodium breadcrumbs using crusts, 1 tablespoon mixed herbs, 1 onion diced, 1 egg to combine together and stuff into cavity.
2. Bake 2 hours at 180º C.
3. Use pan juices to make homemade gravy.

Veggies Roasted in Duck Fat (or use whatever you like to roast in, of course)
- Potato
- Pumpkin
- Parsnip
- Carrot

1. Cut veggies into quarters, slightly larger than bite size.
2. Spray pan with oil and place vegetables in, dollop duck fat around and bake for 1 hour at 180º C.

Looks Like Roast Turkey

- 500g turkey mince
- 1 teaspoon onion powder
- 1 large egg, lightly beaten
- 1 tablespoon olive oil
- ½ teaspoon black pepper
- 1 teaspoon garlic powder
- 1 cup shredded Granny Smith apple, washed with peel on
- ½ cup panko breadcrumbs
- Italian seasoning - McCormick has no-salt, MSG or artificial flavours

1. Mix all ingredients together, place into a bread tin.
2. Bake for approximately 20 minutes.

Slice and serve with roast veggies, cranberry sauce or jelly (very low-sodium content), or make your own cranberry sauce. Lovely served cold with salad.

It Is Roast Turkey (whole bird from scratch) 67mg sodium
- 1 whole turkey (raw or frozen)
- Seasonings and rubs to suit your tastes, e.g. chilli powder, garlic powder, paprika, ground black pepper, onion powder, cayenne, perhaps.

Or *Spice Road Chicken Natural Spice Seasoning.*
- Follow the directions on the packaging of the turkey for cooking times.

Pork & Ham

serves: 6-8 **prep:** 35 minutes **cooking time:** 1 hour 30 minutes

We've been fortunate enough to have a roast pork recipe given to us by Marion, with a Beer Crispy Crackling. A number of members from our Facebook group enjoy it. Every Christmas with my own family (the Simpsons) my dad loved his roast pork with the salty crispy crackling, and his ham. I could eat a small portion of the pork, but not the crackling. He would make Grandma Simpson's apple sauce, adding sugar.

Roast Pork

Roast Pork recipe from *Marion Pasternok - p92*

Ingredients
- 2kg pork belly or shoulder with rind
- 1 onion - chopped
- 1 leek - chopped
- 2 carrots - chopped
- ½ bulb of garlic - crushed
- 1 teaspoon sweet paprika
- pepper
- 1 bottle 330mL - 500mL beer preferable - a Pils or lager

Follow the directions in the method on p92 to create an amazing roast pork with beer crispy crackling.

Grandma Simpson's Apple Sauce

- 4 granny smith apples
- 2 tablespoons raw sugar, ¾ cup of water
- A pinch of cinnamon (optional)

1. Peel the apples, and chop.
2. Add to a saucepan with water and stir in the sugar. Simmer for 15 minutes, stirring occasionally, until the apple sauce is the consistency you would like.

Serve with roast pork.

Grampy's Christmas Ham

Grampy's Christmas ham! My kids loved when my dad dropped around a ham for Christmas. I didn't have the same enthusiasm because of the salt! (my poor salt deprived children!) But I loved that he did that for us. *The Christmas spirit.*

If you love ham but not the salt, research online, there are de-salting methods to reduce the salt content. And I found the following leg hams have less sodium than the usual 1020mg/100g or more.
- *D'orsogna Natural Leg Ham* with no artificial nitrites, to be lower in sodium - 245mg per serving, and
- *DON Premium Honey Leg Ham* roll with 426mg per serving.
- *Bertocchi Salt Reduced Classic Leg Virginia Ham* - 300mg per serving

Sometimes I will have a tiny bit of leg ham, but not enough to spill me over my sodium content of 1,200 - 1,500 max or for the day. Usually my body will tell me whether I can have it or not, by making me feel repelled by it, or any other high-salt or processed foods.

Christmas Lunch Cold Meats

serves: 6 - 8 **prep:** 10 minutes **cooking time:** 0 minutes

Living in Australia gets particularly hot, and some places around the country have a high humidity as well, making it hot and sticky. You'll find some families having a Christmas lunch that consists of cold meats and seafood and salads. And of course, no matter whether you have a hot or cold Christmas lunch, there's backyard cricket and swimming in the pool before Christmas dessert - Julieann

Cold Meats

Cuts of cold home cooked lamb, beef, ham, turkey, and chicken are popular. If you don't already have your own low-sodium go-to for cold meats, you can roast meats listed on the pages before, refrigerate them and slice them on Christmas day. Choose a variety of meats, depending on your tastes and traditions. Some families have a BBQ with salads as well. Sally recommends liberally adding ground pepper on both sides of your steak before BBQing, for more flavour.

Seafood

Salmon, cod, tuna, flounder, snapper, barramundi, sea perch and halibut are low-sodium seafood options. *Raw versions* of prawns, oysters, clams, scallops, mussels are relatively low in sodium. *Flavour your seafood* with herbs, spices and vinegar. Add the juice and zest from lemons, limes and oranges to pack a flavour punch. Serve separately or combine with salads.

Some Salad ideas

Here's just some ideas for you to search for: *Potato Salad*, Roasted Pumpkin Salad with Honey and Balsamic Dressings, *Pumpkin and Spinach Salad*, Roasted Pumpkin and Quinoa Salad, *Couscous Salad*, Green Salad with Mango, *Chicken and Mango Salad*, Pasta Salad with Lentils, Pesto and Beans, *Rice, Cranberry and Sweet Potato Salad*, Lemon Leaf Salad with Sliced Apple, *Apple Salad with Raspberry Dressing*, Prawn Mango and Avocado Salad (buy raw prawns and cook them yourself to control sodium), *Prawn Peach and Goat's Cheese Salad*, Avocado Salad with Orange Vinaigrette, *Cherry and Watermelon Salad with Lime and Mint Syrup*, Low-sodium Apple Walnut Salad, *Strawberry Spinach Salad*, Apple Slaw, *Low-sodium Pulled Pork Chopped Salad*, Turkey Sweet Potato Salad, *Wild Berry Salad with Chocolate Balsamic Dressing*. Look for reduced salt Feta (Olympus), or substitute with Ricotta Cheese for recipes, or use naturally low-sodium cheeses -mozzarella, Swiss cheese, ricotta, goat cheese, or cottage cheese. *I found some delicious low-sodium salad dressings at healthecooks.com.*

Christmas Lunch Salads x2

serves: 6-8 **prep:** 35 minutes **cooking time:** 0 minutes

Sally's sister, Nola, gifted us these two salad recipes, which she always receives requests for. She made them for Sally initially, but are universally popular.

Spinach and Pomegranate Salad

Ingredients

- 1 bag baby spinach leaves, or equivalent fresh
- ½ cup unsalted walnut pieces (or pecans)
- ¼ cup red spanish onion, thinly sliced
- ½ cup pomegranate seeds
- 1 Fuji (or similar) apple, very thinly sliced, with skin on

For balsamic Vinaigrette

- ¾ cup olive oil
- 2 teaspoons honey
- ½ cup balsamic vinegar
- pepper to taste

Optional - In a separate bowl for non-Ménière's guests: ½ cup crumbled feta cheese, or use ricotta cheese instead.

Method

1. Make the vinaigrette dressing first so that it can be poured over after apple is added so apple doesn't brown.
2. Mix all dressing ingredients together and shake vigorously to combine.
3. Wash and dry spinach leaves and place in a salad bowl.
4. Thinly slice red onion. Place onion and walnut pieces in salad bowl.
5. Wash, dry and core apple. Slice very thinly with skin on for colour. Pour dressing over apple and add to salad bowl.
6. Mix in pomegranate seeds.

Optional - Sprinkle on feta cheese or ricotta cheese.

Green Bean Salad

- as many fresh green beans as you like
- as many button mushrooms as you like.
- pine nuts
- fresh ricotta cheese - not wet
- olive oil

Green Bean Salad Method

1. Wash and top and tail beans. Leave full length, and string if required.
2. Slice mushrooms.
3. Blanche beans to soften slightly.
4. Fry mushrooms in olive oil until golden.
5. Place pine nuts in a single layer in a dry skillet. Cook, stirring throughout, on a low-medium heat until they become golden brown and smell quite nutty. Cool.
6. Combine the beans, mushrooms and toasted pine nuts.

Dressing is not generally required due to mushroom and pine nut flavours.

Fig and Cherry Cake

serves: 12 **prep:** 20 minutes **cooking time:** 1 hour - 1 hour 45 minutes

This is a wonderful festive cake which I have made for many years as an alternative to a more traditional Christmas cake. You do need to start it at least four days ahead of time so that the fruit have adequate soaking time. There are non-alcohol versions of the Amaretto and Brandy - you may need to search online for outlets near you, or on-line suppliers) ~ Sally

Ingredients

For the fruit:

- ⅔ cup of Amaretto (non-alcohol version for those who avoid alcohol)
- ⅓ cup Brandy (non-alcohol versions available)
- 1 tablespoon honey
- 165g dried tart cherries (*not* Maraschino cherries)
- 165g golden figs, stemmed and cut into eighths
- 165g golden sultanas

For the batter:

- 120g unsalted butter, softened
- 85g almond paste * (see notes)
- 1 cup white sugar
- 3 large eggs at room temperature
- ½ teaspoon vanilla extract (this is stronger than vanilla essence)
- 140g unbleached white flour * (see notes)

NOTES

I have found almond paste is an American concept and not always available in Australia. You could substitute marzipan, or as I have done, make your own **almond paste:**

- *Mix a cup of almond meal, a cup of icing sugar, ⅔ teaspoon of almond essence and 1 small stiffly beaten egg white until smooth. It is pliable but quite dense. It should form a ball.*
- *Pulse the almond flour a few times to break up any clumps. Add almond essence and pulse to combine. Test to see if it tastes almondy enough to your taste. Add egg white and process for 2 minutes.*
- *If too sticky, add some more almond meal.*
- *Wrap tightly and store in fridge.*

Yes, this uses plain flour, which has sodium. But it is so little that in the totality of the cake it is not all that much.

** The Fig & Cherry cake photo depicts purple figs, which you can use if you can't source golden figs.

Method

1. Four days to one week ahead: Pour amaretto, brandy and honey into a small to medium saucepan. Add the dried fruit, cover and warm over a medium heat until hot (about 3 minutes). Remove from heat and let cool. Refrigerate until ready to make the cake.
2. When ready to make, bring fruit to room temperature and drain. Reserve any liquid for basting. It may have all been absorbed.
3. Heat oven to 170º C.
4. Butter a loaf tin (about 22cm x 11cm). Line it with baking paper, leaving an overhang for removal. I find two strips in opposite directions best for this.
5. Beat butter, almond paste and sugar on a medium to high speed until fluffy and there are no lumps of almond paste (about 3-4 minutes).
6. Beat in eggs one at a time - 30-60 seconds each egg. Beat in vanilla essence.
7. Add two tablespoons of flour and beat briefly. Reserve two tablespoons flour.
8. Add the rest of the flour (minus the two tablespoons reserved), and beat on low for 10 seconds and high for 1 minute.
9. Scrape batter into the centre of the bowl. Add drained fruit to the top. Sprinkle over the remaining flour.
10. Use a spatula and fold in the fruit. Put in prepared tin. Press to eliminate air pockets. Smooth top.
11. Bake 15 minutes then reduce the temperature to 150º C.
12. Bake until the centre has risen slightly and a skewer comes out clean. This should take about 1 hour 40 to 1 hour 45 minutes.
13. Remove from oven and cool for 20-25 minutes. Invert on a wire rack.
14. When cool, brush 2-3 tablespoons of reserved fruit liquid or 1 - 1½ tablespoons of Amaretto and Brandy.
15. Wrap tightly in plastic wrap and store in a cool, dry place for a minimum of 48 hours.
16. If keeping for longer than a week, baste once a week with 1-2 tablespoons of amaretto and brandy.

Julieann's Pavlova

serves: 8 **prep:** 15minutes **cooking time:** 1 hour 15 minutes

Christmas in Australia can be hot and humid and oppressive, so Pavlova is always a welcome dessert on the Christmas table. I've made pavlova at Christmas time for my kids, like forever, as they don't like Christmas pudding with the dried fruit. And I've always made it from scratch~ Julieann

Ingredients

Meringue
- 4 egg whites
- 1 cup caster sugar
- 1 teaspoon white vinegar
- 1 tablespoon cornflour

Pavlova topping

- Dollop cream or whipped thickened cream with a little icing sugar.
- 1 banana
- strawberries
- blueberries
- 2 passionfruit
- 1 mango
- 1 kiwi fruit
- add other fruits of your choice

Method

1. Heat oven to 120º C.
2. On a baking tray, place a sheet of baking paper, and sprinkle it with cornflour. This stops the pavlova from sticking to the baking paper when serving.
3. With an electric mixer, beat egg whites on high speed until stiff.
4. Add caster sugar 2 tablespoons at time, ensuring it is dissolved before adding the next caster sugar tablespoonfuls. Scrape down the sides between adding caster sugar. I always test the meringue mixture with my fingers to check that the sugar is dissolved.
5. Add teaspoon of white vinegar, mixing very slowly.
6. Add tablespoon of cornflour, folding it in.
7. Spoon pavlova mixture in the centre of the baking paper on the baking tray, shaping however you would like it to be shaped. Make sure that it is a high mound, otherwise it becomes a very flat pavlova.
8. Bake in the oven for 1 hour and 15 minutes, opening the oven door when finished to allow it to cool completely.
9. Add cream or yoghurt, and fruit, decorating it with your own artistic style (my kids usually do this part, and I never know how my prized pavlova is going to look!).

I always make a double batch of pavlova, as it disappears before I can get a second serving.

Royal Family Christmas Pudding

serves: 6-8 **prep:** 30 minutes **cooking time:** overnight & 4 hours

This recipe is from a colleague, who made it each year. He claimed it was adapted from the Royal Family's Christmas Pudding. I have since adapted it as low-sodium and alcohol free as possible. If alcohol is not a trigger for you, go ahead and use alcohol. This quantity is enough for a 2.5L pudding bowl ~ Sally

Ingredients

- 150g unsalted butter
- 5 eggs
- 340g currants
- 225g brown sugar
- 170g dates
- 340g sultanas
- 170g raisins
- 170g walnuts or almonds, or a mix
- 113g plain flour
- 113g breadcrumbs (find the lowest sodium bread you can, and crumb yourself, or make some no-salt bread yourself
- 100mL rum or sherry (no-alcohol versions if you need)
- 150mL water
- 2 tablespoons Parisian essence
- 1 rounded teaspoon mixed spice
- ½ rounded teaspoon grated nutmeg
- ¼ teaspoon *Salt Skip* potassium bicarbonate (available from lowsodiumfoods.com.au)
- 1 teaspoon vanilla extract
- 1 teaspoon lemon essence

Method

The pudding can be made weeks or months ahead of time and stored in a cool dry place. It is finished on the day of serving, taking an hour on that day.

1. Cut dates into small pieces and combine with other fruits and rum or sherry and water. Leave to soak for 24 hours.
2. Sift plain flour, potassium bicarb and spices three times.
3. Cream butter and brown sugar.
4. Add eggs to creamed mixture one at a time, beating well after each addition.
5. Add the Parisian essence, lemon essence and vanilla extract.
6. Gently fold in breadcrumbs and then fold in flour.
7. Add the fruit and nuts last, and mix well until combined. Mixture will be very moist.
8. Grease a pudding basin and place a circle of baking paper in the bottom.
9. Cover the basin with its lid.
10. Stand the pudding basin on egg rings in a large saucepan/ boiler so the pudding will not burn if the pot accidentally burns dry.
11. Steam in the large saucepan/boiler for 4 hours, topping up the water level with hot water as it evaporates.
12. On the day of use, pour two tablespoons of rum or sherry over the top of the pudding, replace the cover and steam for another hour. *Serve hot with custard.*

Individual Rhubarb and Apple Muesli Muffins

serves: 6-8 **prep:** 30 minutes **cooking time:** 20-30 minutes

I have never written this recipe down; I just made it up as I went along, and do every time I make it. Therefore, if the quantities seem a little scant or over, feel free to adjust! ~ Sally

Ingredients

- 2 cups of plain muesli. I like Carman's Toasted Original, Fruit Free which is 18mg/100g sodium. Or you can make your own muesli
- *Optional*: ¼ cup coconut flakes added to the muesli
- 150g unsalted butter, softened but not melted. Leave overnight out of the fridge and it should reach the right consistency
- 4 stalks of rhubarb, washed and cut into 2 cm lengths
- 1 granny smith apple, quartered and cut into very thin slices
- A few drops of vanilla extract (extract is stronger and more flavoursome than vanilla essence)
- 1 teaspoon of balsamic vinegar
- plain Greek style (thick) yoghurt

Method

Equipment
Large size silicon or paper patty pans or muffin moulds. *I use individual ones* because they can be served and eaten straight from the pan without anything falling out.

1. Rub butter into muesli and coconut mix until forms a ball which holds together.
2. Spoon a layer of the muesli/butter mix into the bottom of a patty pan - about 1cm.
3. Place rhubarb, apple slices, balsamic vinegar and vanilla extract into a saucepan and gently bring to boil and cook until rhubarb and apple are soft. Keep a close eye on it, stirring occasionally, to ensure that it does not burn. If it looks too dry, add a few drops of water.
4. Spoon into the patty pans on top of the muesli base until about 1cm from the top.
5. Add another layer of the muesli/butter mix, and mould into a slightly rounded dome. Can sprinkle some more coconut slivers on now.
6. Cook in fan-forced oven about 180º C (non fan-forced about 200º C) until golden brown.

Best served with a large dollop of plain yoghurt. Eat straight from the patty pan. *I have eaten this for breakfast, as a mid-morning or afternoon snack, or for dessert.*

Christmas Shortbread

makes: 24 **prep:** 20 minutes **cooking time:** 15-20 minutes

Claire and I are in the kitchen with our reindeer antlers on making shortbread. Bing Crosby Christmas carols are trying to unsuccessfully drown out my tinnitus. We both love making Christmas Shortbread. It's like playing with play dough when Claire was little. I leave the decorating to Claire, and she always makes a vertigo swirl on one, just for me ~ Julieann

Ingredients

- 225g unsalted butter, coarsely chopped
- ½ cup caster sugar
- ⅔ cup rice flour
- 1½ cups plain flour - sifted

Optional
- add slivered almonds, pistachios, dry cranberries or chocolate chips.
- melted white or milk chocolate
- Christmas sprinkles
- pure icing mixture

Let It Snow
2 tablespoons each of sifted icing sugar and arrowroot flour

Method

1. Preheat oven to 160⁰ C.
2. Place baking paper on an oven tray.
3. Use your fingertips to rub together butter, flours and sugar until it looks like breadcrumbs.
4. Remove from bowl and place on a lightly floured surface and knead until smooth. *If you are adding slivered almonds, pistachios, dry cranberries or chocolate chips, add these now.*
5. On baking paper on the bench, use a rolling pin to roll the dough until it is about 1cm thick.
6. Use Christmas cookie cutters to cut shapes, and place onto the tray.
7. Place into the over for 15-20 minutes until golden.

Dust with *Let It Snow,* or drizzles of melted white or milk chocolate, or Christmas sprinkles.

Serve with tea of coffee, or not. Enjoy!

Christmas Gingernut Ripple Cake

serves: 8 **prep:** 15 minutes **refrigeration time:** 6-8 hours

Traditionally, I've always made a Choc Ripple Cake for my kids as they always request it at Christmas time when they come home. For us, them coming home always involves Mum cooking their favourite meals. They always get their wish and this way I can now enjoy sharing a dessert with them low-sodium wise. Lots of family memories around the Christmas table ~ Kim

Ingredients

- 1 packet of Leda Gingernut biscuits (low-sodium)
- 600mL thickened cream
- 2 teaspoons vanilla essence
- sugar to taste
- grated chocolate (your choice) to decorate

Method

1. Whip cream, vanilla and sugar until stiff peaks form.
2. Put a thick layer of cream on one side of biscuit and sandwich to another one, repeat until all biscuits are joined together with cream. Shape into a log shape as you work. Cover thickly with remaining cream, ensuring all biscuits are covered, cover with cling wrap and place in fridge for approx. 6-8 hours so biscuits soften.
3. When ready to serve, sprinkle grated chocolate over to decorate.
4. Cut on the diagonal.

Enjoy

Fruit Christmas Tree

Serves: 6-8 **prep:** 15 minutes **cooking time:** 0 minutes

One of my kids isn't a big dessert eater, and prefers fruit instead (a dream child?). So I make a fruit Christmas tree just for him. It's quick and easy. Sometimes I make a standing up version, and other times I make the base Christmas tree shape using watermelon wedges, and then just place the other fruits on top. Also, I have popped my mother-in-law's homemade custard here. It's the best! ~ Julieann

Ingredients

- watermelon
- blueberries
- strawberries
- pineapple
- raspberries
- banana
- kiwi fruit
- rockmelon
- grapes
- blackberries/mulberries
- red apple (optional)

Centre of tree for stabilisation
- large apple
- super long thick carrot
- toothpicks

Method

1. Using a star shape cutter, make watermelon stars. Do this also for kiwi and rockmelon if you like.
2. Cut pineapple into chunks.
3. Slice banana and coat them with either orange/lemon or lime juice to stop them browning.
4. Cut red apple into thin wedges, if using.

Build it

1. Large apple - slice the ends off, so that it sits level, then make a core in the middle to house a super long, thick carrot.
2. Using toothpicks, insert them into the carrot, building the branches of the tree.
3. Place fruit onto the toothpicks, finishing with a star shaped fruit on the top.

Nan's Homemade Custard

4 eggs, 1 teaspoon butter, 4 cups milk, ½ cup white sugar, 3 tablespoons cornstarch, 1 tablespoon vanilla extract.

Put butter, milk and vanilla into a saucepan and simmer over medium heat (don't let it boil). Whisk eggs, sugar and cornstarch in a small bowl until the sugar dissolves. Add to the saucepan slowly, stirring until it thickens.

Can be served warm or cold.

My Christmas Recipes

4 Week Eating Plan

We've written a *4 week meal plan* for you, based on recipes from this cookbook. The difficulty with doing this is we don't know your dietary needs besides low-sodium, so if there is *diary* or *nuts* or *gluten* or *sugar* etc that you don't tolerate, cross it out and *write your own* food preferences in. In fact, if there are *any foods* you dislike, *cross it out* and add you own.

Also, you *don't have to* eat everything on the weekly plan. Eat what *suits you* each day. *Freeze leftovers.*

The *rationale* behind the food planner is to help take *stress* off you for meal planning. You know, that constant *looking* for what you can and can't eat. And also, if you are *unwell* and can't cook for yourself, we've tried to make it easy for your *carer* to be able to *use this book* and *create* low-sodium meals for you.

We've also added *four blank weekly meal planner pages,* so you can add *the foods* that suit your body and needs best.

What did the strawberry say to its crush?
I'm berry fond of you.

What was the math teacher's favourite dessert?
Pie.

What did the hamburger name her daughter?
Patty.

Food Planner Week 1

Week 1	Breakfast	Morning Tea	Lunch	Afternoon Tea	Dinner
Sunday	Poached eggs with smashed avocado and cooked tomato p2	Fruit with yoghurt	Salad wrap p19	Dried apricots Sunrice Thin Rice Cakes	Sally's Pasta Ragu (aka Spag Bol) p83
drinks					
Monday	Acai bowl p6	No-salt crackers with slices of apple	Potato cooked in microwave filled with etc p36	Raw veggies with dip - carrots, etc	Aunty Jude's Perky Pumpkin Soup p63
drinks					
Tuesday	Scrambled eggs p4	Arnott's Snack Right Oaty Bites (Cocoa and Oat)	No add salt tuna mixed with sour cream and dill p19	Unsalted nuts Fruit	Shepherd's Pie p86
drinks					
Wednesday	Honey yoghurt, unsalted nuts p3	Low-sodium rice cakes with hard boiled egg	Low salt cheese and avocado on low salt crackers p18	Frozen fruit smoothie	Roast chicken p148
drinks					
Thursday	⅓ cup quick oats, mashed banana, 1 egg, etc	Fruit	Homemade flat bread wrap with avocado etc p19	Celery sticks with peanut butter.	Beef or Pork or Veal or Chicken Schnitz p89
drinks					
Friday	Poached egg on avocado with cottage cheese p5	Guacamole and salt-free corn chips	Pasta salad p21, 27	Sliced apples dipped in low-sodium peanut butter	Fakeaway Nights - Honey Chicken p72
drinks					
Saturday	Porridge with nuts and blueberries	Chocolate Coconut Go To Snacks p46	Minestrone soup p64	Toast with banana and cinnamon	Slow Cooked Lamb Shanks p84
drinks					

Food Planner Week 2

Week 2	Breakfast	Morning Tea	Lunch	Afternoon Tea	Dinner
Sunday	Acai bowl p6	Loaded rice cakes p44 Fruit	Salad and poached chicken, home-made dressing p20	The Carrot Bread of Hidden Apple p47	Italian Lamb with Balsamic Glaze p85
drinks					
Monday	Mini quiche bites p6	Hummus and veggie sticks p49	Avocado. Add tomato, chicken, lettuce all stacked p21	Fruit Unsalted nuts	Chicken & Veggie Soup p67
drinks					
Tuesday	Boiled eggs and avocado on homemade bread	No-salt crackers with slices of apple	Fruit salad	Grandad's Peanut Biscuits p50	Greek Lamb and Salad p90
drinks					
Wednesday	pancakes with whipped egg whites p6	Frozen fruit smoothie	Lettuce leaf wrap p21	Unsalted nuts	Butter Chicken p77
drinks					
Thursday	⅓ cup quick oats, mashed banana, etc p5	Fruit Unsalted nuts	Hemp Seed Tabbouleh p33	Mini Blueberry Muffins p51	Fish Tacos p103
drinks					
Friday	Poached egg on avocado with cottage cheese p5	Yoghurt	Rice cakes with toppings p35	Fruit	Beef Nachos p87
drinks					
Saturday	Pancakes with zucchini or carrot p4	Toast with banana and cinnamon.	Corn Chowder p27	Raw veggies with dip	Chicken Wraps p80
drinks					

Food Planner Week 3

Week 3	Breakfast	Morning Tea	Lunch	Afternoon Tea	Dinner
Sunday	Poached eggs, smashed avocado and cooked tomato p2	Date and Pumpkin Loaf p48	Small tin of tuna, beans, salad etc p21	Fruit	Chicken and Mushroom Risotto p70
drinks					
Monday	Porridge with nuts and blueberries	Unsalted nuts	Yoghurt and fruit	Low-sodium rice cakes with hard boiled egg	Calypso Beef p88
drinks					
Tuesday	Scrambled eggs p4	Fruit	Zucchini pancakes p22		Mini pizzas p96
drinks					
Wednesday	Açai bowl of fresh berries, banana etc p4, 6	Frozen fruit smoothie	Refreshing apple and cheese on bread p31 & 24	Unsalted nuts	Apricot Chicken p78, 79
drinks					
Thursday	⅓ cup quick oats, mashed banana, 1 egg, dash cinnamon then a few blueberries.	No-salt crackers with slices of apple	Pasta & Pesto p34	yoghurt	homemade hamburgers p58
drinks					
Friday	Poached egg on avocado with cottage cheese p5	Loaded rice cakes p44	Jacket Potato p36	Fruit	Cantonese Chicken p75
drinks					
Saturday	Mini quiche bites p6	Fruit Unsalted nuts	My Favourite Salad Lunch p30	Raw veggies with dip	Roast Pork p92 or Vegetarian Mini Pizzas p96
drinks					

Food Planner Week 4

Week 4	Breakfast	Morning Tea	Lunch	Afternoon Tea	Dinner
Sunday	Acai bowl p6	Homemade muffins	Sandwich Stack p31	Fruit	Stroganoff Meatballs p93
drinks					
Monday	Mini quiche bites p6	Loaded rice cakes p44	Zucchini, Mushroom and Ricotta Pasta Sauce p34	No-salt crackers with slices of apple	Brown Rice and Tuna Salad p99
drinks					
Tuesday	Boiled eggs and avocado on homemade bread	Fruit Unsalted nuts	Rice cakes with toppings p35	Yoghurt	Pumpkin & Ricotta Lasagne p95
drinks					
Wednesday	Pancakes with whipped egg whites p6	Frozen fruit smoothie	Change it up Salad p32	Popcorn and unsalted nuts	Chicken Vadouvan recipe p76
drinks					
Thursday	⅓ cup quick oats, mashed banana, 1 egg, dash cinnamon then a few blueberries	Fruit	Tuna/Salmon Garden Salad p35	Toast with honey and peanut butter	Steak sandwiches p59
drinks					
Friday	Poached egg on avocado with cottage cheese. p5	Fruit Unsalted nuts	Nick's Butter Chicken p26	Loaded rice cakes p44	Thai Salad p88
drinks					
Saturday	Pancakes with zucchini or carrot p4	Mini Blueberry Muffins p51	Singapore Noodles p28	Fruit with yoghurt	Sweet Chilli Chicken Rice p74
drinks					

My Food Planner Week 1

Week 1	Breakfast	Morning Tea	Lunch	Afternoon Tea	Dinner
Sunday					
drinks					
Monday					
drinks					
Tuesday					
drinks					
Wednesday					
drinks					
Thursday					
drinks					
Friday					
drinks					
Saturday					
drinks					

My Food Planner Week 2

Week 2	Breakfast	Morning Tea	Lunch	Afternoon Tea	Dinner
Sunday					
drinks					
Monday					
drinks					
Tuesday					
drinks					
Wednesday					
drinks					
Thursday					
drinks					
Friday					
drinks					
Saturday					
drinks					

My Food Planner Week 3

Week 3	Breakfast	Morning Tea	Lunch	Afternoon Tea	Dinner
Sunday					
drinks					
Monday					
drinks					
Tuesday					
drinks					
Wednesday					
drinks					
Thursday					
drinks					
Friday					
drinks					
Saturday					
drinks					

My Food Planner Week 4

Week 4	Breakfast	Morning Tea	Lunch	Afternoon Tea	Dinner
Sunday					
drinks					
Monday					
drinks					
Tuesday					
drinks					
Wednesday					
drinks					
Thursday					
drinks					
Friday					
drinks					
Saturday					
drinks					

Nutrition & Exercise

When you have *Meniere's*, and in the lead up to a *vertigo attack*, in the *cluster of attacks*, or exhausted after *vertigo*, the last thing you want to do is exercise. The thing is, exercise is *terribly important* for people with vestibular disorders. Exercise *improves your balance*, helps the *brain* adapt to confusing signals, reduces the *risk of falls*, helps with *brain fog* and *stress*, and *improves blood circulation* systemically, including the *inner ear*. Let's be real. Exercise can be a *challenge*. But by *having a go*, you've already *won*! *Start slowly* and *build up* in duration and repetitions. *Have someone with you* to be on the safe side. Walking. Rowing machine. Cycling, or exercise bike. Gym. Swimming. *Keep a diary*. Each time you exercise, even marching up and down inside the house, you are *on the road to success*.

And please, after a vertigo attack, give yourself time to recover, however that looks for you. *Be kind to yourself*! We never asked for this life-changing vestibular disorder that turns our world upside down.

Read *Phillip's* rebound back to well-being with exercise & low-sodium food.

My favorite exercise?
Spin class, because it's wheel-y good for you!

Why was the spin class teacher arrested?
For cycle-logical manipulation.

Have you heard about the spinning class at the gym?
It's a total revolution.

Phillip's story

When I was diagnosed with Ménière's disease, *everything changed*. The vertigo, the ringing, the fatigue - it all hit hard. At first, I just wanted to make it through each day without spinning out.

Being told to lower my sodium intake started as a medical recommendation but soon became a turning point. I began counting calories, reducing carbs, and walking at least 10,000 steps a day. I set myself a goal to improve my cardiovascular fitness - to run five kilometres in under five minutes per kilometre, *a military standard*.

Seven months later, I was running at 4 minutes and 37 seconds per kilometre and had dropped 35kg. From there, I increased my calories and carbs, focused on protein, and returned to the gym six days a week using a push–pull–legs training split. Over the following five months, I gained six kilograms of lean muscle.

Managing Ménière's through nutrition taught me that food isn't just fuel - it's part of the recovery. My contribution to this book is a reflection of that lesson: that low-sodium doesn't have to mean low flavour, and that small changes can lead to big transformations! Over the next few pages, I share a small sample of meal recipes.

Supplements - Whey Protein Isolate, Creatine, BCAA + EAA, Citrulline Malate - under the supervision of my trainer and GP.

Disclaimer - My lifestyle change is for informational purposes only and isn't medical or professional advice. Seek professional assistance before hand if considering supplements.

Breakfast

Blueberry Protein Overnight Oats

serves: 1 **prep:** 10 minutes **cooking time:** overnight

A super easy breakfast I make the night before - high in protein and great on training mornings. Tip: Sometimes I top it with a spoon of Greek yoghurt or a few almonds for crunch.

Ingredients

- ½ cup rolled oats
- 1 scoop vanilla protein powder
- 1 tablespoon chia seeds
- ¾ cup unsweetened almond milk
- ¼ cup blueberries (fresh or frozen)
- dash of cinnamon

Macros (approx): Calories: 365 kcal, Protein: 33g, Carbs: 40g, Fat: 8g, Sodium: 95mg

Method

1. Mix all ingredients in a jar or container.
2. Stir well, cover, and refrigerate overnight.
3. In the morning, give it a quick stir and add extra milk if needed.

Savoury Egg White Scramble

Tip: Sometimes I add a sprinkle of smoked paprika or chilli flakes for flavour. Serves 1.

Ingredients

- 4 egg whites (or 2 whole eggs + 2 whites)
- ½ cup chopped capsicum
- ¼ cup diced onion
- handful of baby spinach
- 2 mushrooms, sliced
- black pepper, garlic powder, and herbs of choice

Macros (approx): Calories: 210 kcal, Protein: 27g, Carbs: 6g, Fat: 8g, Sodium: 160mg

Method

1. Lightly spray a pan with olive oil.
2. Sauté onion, mushroom, and capsicum for a few minutes.
3. Add spinach and pour in eggs.
4. Stir gently until cooked through.

Snacks

Rice Cake Snacks Three Ways

serves: 1 **prep:** 10 minutes **cooking time:** 0 minutes

Quick, crunchy, and low sodium. This is a perfect quick snack that feels like dessert.
Tip: Add a drizzle of sugar-free maple syrup if you've got a sweet tooth.

Ingredients

- rice cakes (Ceres Organics - *Low Sodium Foods Australia*)
- almond butter + banana slices
- hummus (unsalted) + cucumber
- cottage cheese (low-sodium) + blueberries

Macros (per rice cake, average): Calories: 120–140 kcal, Protein: 6–10g, Carbs: 10–15g, Fat: 4–6g, Sodium: 60–100mg

Method

1. Slather your rice cake with any of these toppings. It will keep you going.

Greek Yoghurt Protein Bowl

serves: 1 **prep:** 5 minutes **cooking time:** 0 minutes

Ingredients

- ½ cup plain Greek yoghurt
- 1 scoop vanilla or chocolate protein powder
- ¼ cup berries
- 1 teaspoon chia seeds or crushed almonds

Macros (approx): Calories: 230 kcal, Protein: 32g, Carbs: 12g, Fat: 5g, Sodium: 85mg

Method

1. Mix yoghurt and protein powder until smooth.
2. Top with berries and chia seeds.

Lunch

Chicken & Quinoa Power Bowl

serves: 1 **prep:** 30 minutes **cooking time:** 30 minutes

A simple meal prep option - keeps me full and is great post-gym.
Tip: Keeps in the fridge for 3 days and tastes even better cold.

Ingredients

- 1 cup cooked quinoa
- 150g grilled chicken breast
- ½ cup roasted pumpkin or sweet potato
- handful of spinach or kale
- 1 tablespoon olive oil
- juice of ½ lemon
- crushed garlic and herbs to taste

Macros (approx): Calories: 480 kcal, Protein: 43g, Carbs: 38g, Fat: 15g, Sodium: 115mg

Method

1. Combine quinoa, veggies, and chicken in a bowl.
2. Whisk olive oil, lemon juice, and garlic to make a quick dressing.
3. Pour over and toss well.

Turkey Lettuce Wraps

Light, crunchy, and packed with protein. Tip: A sprinkle of sesame seeds adds crunch without the sodium.

serves: 1 **prep:** 15 minutes **cooking time:** 15 minutes

Ingredients

- 200g lean turkey mince
- 1 small carrot, grated
- ¼ cup diced mushrooms
- 1 teaspoon crushed garlic
- 1 teaspoon grated ginger
- 1 teaspoon rice vinegar
- cos lettuce leaves

Macros (approx): Calories: 310 kcal, Protein: 42g, Carbs: 6g, Fat: 12g, Sodium: 120mg

Method

1. Cook turkey mince in a non-stick pan until browned.
2. Add garlic, ginger, carrot, and mushrooms.
3. Stir in rice vinegar and cook for another minute.
4. Spoon into lettuce leaves and wrap.

Dinner

Lemon & Herb Baked Salmon

serves: 1 **prep:** 10 minutes **cooking time:** 15 - 20 minutes

High in omega-3s and one of my go-tos for an easy dinner.
Tip: Add crushed almonds on top for extra crunch.

Ingredients

- 1 salmon fillet (150–180g)
- 1 tablespoon olive oil
- juice of ½ lemon
- 1 teaspoon minced garlic
- fresh dill or parsley
- black pepper

Method

1. Preheat oven to 180°C.
2. Mix olive oil, lemon juice, garlic, and herbs.
3. Pour over salmon and bake for 15–20 minutes.

Serve with steamed greens and roasted baby potatoes.

Macros (approx): Calories: 420 kcal, Protein: 38g, Carbs: 6g, Fat: 25g, Sodium: 90mg

Low-Sodium Cottage Pie with Cauliflower Mash

Comfort food, minus the salt. Tip: Swap half the cauliflower for potato if you prefer a creamier mash.

serves: 1 **prep:** 10 minutes **cooking time:** 30 minutes

Ingredients

- 300g extra-lean beef mince
- 1 small onion, diced
- 1 carrot, chopped
- ½ cup peas
- 2 tablespoons no-salt tomato paste
- 2 cups cauliflower florets
- 2 tablespoons Greek yoghurt
- black pepper, thyme, garlic powder

Macros (approx): Calories: 465 kcal, Protein: 46g, Carbs: 20g, Fat: 20g, Sodium: 175mg

Method

1. Boil cauliflower until soft, then mash with Greek yoghurt and pepper.
2. In a pan, cook mince and onion until browned.
3. Add carrots, peas, tomato paste, and herbs; simmer 5–10 minutes.
4. Spoon mixture into a baking dish, top with mash, and bake at 180°C for 20 minutes.

Dinner continued

High-Protein Chicken Burrito Bowl

serves: 1 **prep:** 15 minutes **cooking time:** 15 minutes

My go-to when I want something that feels like takeaway but fits my macros.
Tip: Add coriander or jalapeño for extra flavour (both naturally low in sodium).

Ingredients

- 150g grilled chicken breast
- ½ cup brown rice (cooked)
- ¼ cup no-salt black beans (rinsed)
- ¼ cup corn kernels (no-salt added)
- ½ avocado, diced
- ½ tomato, chopped
- juice of ½ lime
- chilli powder, garlic powder, paprika

Method

1. Layer rice, beans, corn, and chicken in a bowl.
2. Top with avocado, tomato, and lime juice.
3. Sprinkle with spices and toss before eating.

Macros (approx): Calories: 510 kcal, Protein: 48g, Carbs: 35g, Fat: 18g, Sodium: 140mg

Exercise

Before you start any exercises, please check with your doctor to make sure that it's safe for you to exercise.

Exercise is terribly important for people with vestibular disorders. Exercise improves your balance, helps the brain adapt to confusing signals, reduces the risk of falls, helps with brain fog and stress, and improves blood circulation systemically, including the inner ear.

But exercise can be a challenge. But by having a go, you've already won!
- Start slowly and build up in duration and repetitions.
- Have someone with you to be on the safe side when you know that you aren't at your best.

If you can't make it to a gym, or you don't want to, you can still exercise at home, or while you are out and about. *Here's some ideas.* **Also research exercises that will suit your situation.**
- Walking at home, in your neighbourhood etc. *When I walk, I make sure I am walking on flat surfaces to make sure I don't fall over, and I also walk during the day as my balance is not as good at night - Julieann.*
- Rowing machine.
- Cycling if you can.
- Exercise bike – a safer option if you have trouble with your balance.
- Swimming.
- Step ups. Stepping up onto a step and down again.
- Planking. Try to hold for 30 seconds, then increase the length of time.
- Push-ups.
- Jogging up and down on the spot.
- Lunges (hold on to something for balance).
- Heel raises – standing flat on your feet, legs slightly apart, then lift both of your heels off the floor. Hold on to something like a table or chair for balance.
- Squats.
- Wall push ups. Siting in a chair and stand.
- Lifting your knees to touch your hands held out waist height.
- Seated forward punches – sitting in a chair, make fists with your hands and push your fists forward one at a time.
- Pilates.

Keep a diary.

Each time you exercise, even marching up and down inside the house, you are on the road to success.

My Exercise Plan

Index

Information
- Adding Flavour with Rubs, Spices & Herbs vii, viii, ix, x, xi, xii, 130, 131,132, 133
- Exercise and Gym p173
- Foods that Fight Inflammation v
- Grab & Go vi
- Measurement Conversion Page xiv
- Ménière's Disease & Salt i
- Reducing your sodium after having too much salty food vi
- Salt Substitutes iv
- Salt vs Sodium ii
- Sugar Alternatives iii

4 Week Eating Plan 163
- Food Planner Week 1 164
- Food Planner Week 2 165
- Food Planner Week 3 166
- Food Planner Week 4 167

BBQ 163
BBQ Rubs & Marinades 130, 131, 132, 133
Salad Dressings 134, 135

Beef, Lamb, Pork Dinner 86
- Beef Nachos 87
- Beef or Pork or Veal or Chicken Schnitz & Parmi 89
- Calypso Beef 88
- Greek Lamb and Salad 90
- Italian Lamb with Balsamic Glaze 85
- Lamb – Method 91
- Roast Pork with Beer Crispy Crackling 92
- Sally's Pasta Ragu (aka Spag Bol) 83
- Shepherd's Pie 86
- Slow Cooked Lamb Shanks 84
- Stroganoff Pork Meatballs 93
- Thai Salad 88

Bread
- Homemade bread 24
- *No-salt* Bread (flat bread) 23

Breakfast 1, 2, 3, 4, 5, 6

Chicken Dinner
- Apricot Chicken - 4 Ways 78, 79
- Butter Chicken 77
- Cantonese Chicken 75
- Chicken and Mushroom Risotto 70
- Chicken Sausage Rolls 73
- Chicken Vadouvan Recipe 76
- Chicken with Ras el hanout 69
- Chicken Wraps 80
- Crumbed Chicken Fillets with Capsicum Sauce 81
- Fakeaway Nights - Honey Chicken 72
- Sweet Chilli Chicken Rice 74

Christmas
- Christmas 139, 140, 141
- Christmas Day Menu Cold 142
- Christmas Day Menu Roast 143
- Grandma Simpson's Apple Sauce 149
- Pork & Ham 149
- Roast Chicken & Turkey 148
- Roast Lamb, Beef & Vegetables 147
- Roast Vegetables 147

Index continued

- Slow Cooked Roast Lamb & Veggies 146
- Spinach and Pomegranate Salad 151

Christmas desserts
- Christmas Shortbread 157
- Claire's Gingerbread 145
- Fig and Cherry Cake 152
- Fruit Christmas Tree 159
- Fruit Mince Pies 145
- Gingernut Ripple Cake 158
- Individual Rhubarb and Apple Muesli Muffins 156
- Julieann's Pavlova 154
- Reindeer Droppings (how uncouth ~ Chocolate Truffles) 144
- Royal Family Christmas Pudding 155
- Rumbles (misheard Rumballs thanks Ménière's) 144

Christmas Lunch Cold 142
- Christmas Lunch Cold Meats 150
- Green Bean Salad 151
- Spinach and Pomegranate Salad 151

Christmas Lunch Hot 143
- Grandma Simpson's Apple Sauce 149
- Pork & Ham 149
- Roast Chicken & Turkey 148
- Roast Lamb, Beef & Vegetables 147
- Roast Menu
- Roast Vegetables 147
- Slow Cooked Roast Lamb & Veggies 146

Dessert 107, 108, 109,
- Apple Pie 114
- Cumquat (or Orange) and Almond Cake 110
- Gluten Free Lemon Polenta Cake 112
- Pumpkin Cheesecake 111
- Quark Cheesecake 115
- Spring Fruit Panna Cotta 113

Dinner 55, 56, 57, 58, 59

Drinks throughout the Day 14, 15
- My Drinks Throughout the Day 15

Feeling Snackish 41, 42, 43, 44, 45
- Chocolate Coconut Go To Snacks 46
- Date and Pumpkin Loaf 48
- Grandad's Peanut Biscuits 50
- Hummus 49
- Mini Blueberry Muffins 51
- The Carrot Bread of Hidden Apple 47

Grab & Go vii

Homemade Sauces 60

Lunch 17, 18, 19, 20, 21
- Change it up Salad 32
- Corn Chowder 37
- Hemp Seed Tabbouleh 33
- Homemade Bread 24
- Jacket Potatoes ~ 3 Ways 36
- Lemon Pepper Chicken with Risoni
- Salad 25
- My Favourite Salad Lunch 30
- My Lunches 38, 39

Index continued

- Nick's Butter Chicken 26
- *No-salt* Bread 23
- Pasta & Pesto 34
- Pasta Salad 27
- Rice Cake Toppings 35
- Salt Free French Onion Soup Mix 29
- Sandwiches 31
- Simple, long life Salad Dressing 29
- Singapore Noodles 28
- Summertime Lunch 37
- Tuna/Salmon Garden Salad 35
- Zucchini Pancakes 22
- Zucchini, Mushroom and Ricotta Pasta Sauce 34

Mindset & Gratitude i

My 4 Week Food Planner 168
- My Food Planner Week 1 168
- My Food Planner Week 2 169
- My Food Planner Week 3 170
- My Food Planner Week 4 170

My Exercise Plan 180, 181

Nutrition & Exercise 173
- Breakfast 175
- Dinner 178, 179
- Lunch 177
- Snacks 176

Panic! I've had too much salt! viii

Party Food 119, 120, 121, 122, 123
- Dizzy Fairy Bread 124
- Vanilla Swirl Cupcakes aka Vertigo Cupcakes 125

Seafood 98
- Brown Rice and Tuna Salad 99
- Cod and Lemon 102
- Crumbed Chicken Fillets with Capsicum Sauce 81
- Fish Tacos 103
- Prawn and Mussels Pasta Sauce 100
- Tuna/Salmon Garden Salad 35

Seasonings and Rubs
- Beef, Pork & Lamb Seasonings & Rubs mix xi
- Chicken Seasonings & Rubs ix
- Seafood Seasonings xiii
- Vegetable Seasonings xiv

Soups 63
- Aunty Jude's Perky Pumpkin Soup 63
- Chicken & Veggie Soup 67
- Gluepot Lentil and Pumpkin Soup 66
- Sally's Minestrone Soup 64

That morning liquid... 9, 10, 11, 12
- My Morning Liquid 13

Vegetables 94
- Pumpkin & Ricotta Lasagne 95
- Roast Vegetables 147
- Vegan Pesto 97
- Vegetarian Mini Pizzas 96

Acknowledgements

Sally, Kim, Anne, Phillip and Julieann would like to acknowledge *everyone who contributed* to our Ménière's Low-Sodium Cookbook, whether it be by submitting recipes, or taking part in our online Ménière's group conversations. It takes a village, and we couldn't have done it without you.

Julieann would also like to thank *Professor Jose Antonio Lopez Escamez* (Professor of Meniere disease Neuroscience, *The University of Sydney* Faculty of Medicine and Health, School of Medical Sciences) for providing her with his current genetic research into Ménière's disease which states, "The implementation of genetic and cytokine testing for MD in clinical practice will revolutionise the diagnosis of MD by facilitating personalised treatment strategies. In the near future, patients will benefit from gene therapy and immune phenotype-based treatments including anti-IgE/IL-4R drugs (dupilumab, omalizumab) in IgE/type2 cytokine patients, or TNF-α or IL-1 ß blockers (adalimumab, anakinra) in autoimmune / autoinflammatory patients."

4 November, 2025: https://www.entandaudiologynews.com/features/audiology-features/post/genetic-foundations-of-ménière-s-disease-changing-the-game

Julieann (Ménière's since 1995) also recommends that you have a *definitive diagnosis from an ENT* for your Ménière's to ensure you have the best treatment options for you. There are conditions that mimic the symptoms Ménière's, and can be helped with cervical adjustments, TMJ (temporomandibular joint) alignment, the Epley maneuver for misaligned crystals in the inner ear, or medications for vestibular migraines, labyrinthitis, vestibular neuronitis, acoustic neuroma, stroke, multiple sclerosis and certain infections, etc.

Meniere's Disease
Vertigo. Hearing loss. Tinnitus.
Debilitating.
Life changing.
hope

The spark of hope can never be extinguished.

www.ingramcontent.com/pod-product-compliance
Lightning Source LLC
Chambersburg PA
CBHW061122070526
44583CB00028B/3365